Burton Raffel has taught English and comparative literature at universities in the United States, Israel, and Canada. His books include translations of *Beowulf*, *The Complete Poetry and Prose of Chairil Anwar*, *From the Vietnamese*, *Ten Centuries of Poetry*, *The Complete Poetry of Osip Emilevich Mandelstram* (with Alla Burago), *Poems from the Old English*, and *The Annotated Milton*; critical studies including *Introduction to Poetry*, *How to Read a Poem*, *The Development of Modern Indonesian Poetry*, and *The Forked Tongue: A Study of the Translation Process*; and *Mia Poems*, a volume of his own poetry. Mr. Raffel practiced law on Wall Street and taught in the Ford Foundation's English Language Teacher Training Project in Indonesia.

Roberta Frank, Marie Borroff Professor of English at Yale University, works in the area of Old Norse and Old English language and literature. She has written widely on *Beowulf*, including the recent "A Scandal in Toronto: *The Dating of Beowulf* a Quarter-Century On" (2007).

BEOWULF

Translated and with an Introduction by
BURTON RAFFEL
and with a New Afterword by
ROBERTA FRANK

SIGNET CLASSICS

SIGNET CLASSICS
Published by New American Library, a division of
Penguin Group (USA) Inc., 375 Hudson Street,
New York, New York 10014, USA
Penguin Group (Canada), 90 Eglinton Avenue East, Suite 700, Toronto,
Ontario M4P 2Y3, Canada (a division of Pearson Penguin Canada Inc.)
Penguin Books Ltd., 80 Strand, London WC2R 0RL, England
Penguin Ireland, 25 St. Stephen's Green, Dublin 2,
Ireland (a division of Penguin Books Ltd.)
Penguin Group (Australia), 250 Camberwell Road, Camberwell, Victoria 3124,
Australia (a division of Pearson Australia Group Pty. Ltd.)
Penguin Books India Pvt. Ltd., 11 Community Centre, Panchsheel Park,
New Delhi - 110 017, India
Penguin Group (NZ), 67 Apollo Drive, Rosedale, North Shore 0632,
New Zealand (a division of Pearson New Zealand Ltd.)
Penguin Books (South Africa) (Pty.) Ltd., 24 Sturdee Avenue,
Rosebank, Johannesburg 2196, South Africa

Penguin Books Ltd., Registered Offices:
80 Strand, London WC2R 0RL, England

Published by Signet Classics, an imprint of New American Library, a division
of Penguin Group (USA) Inc. Previously published in a Mentor edition.

First Signet Classics Printing, September 1999
First Signet Classics Printing (Frank Afterword), June 2008

10 9 8 7

Copyright © Burton Raffel, 1963
Afterword copyright © Roberta Frank, 2008
All rights reserved

 REGISTERED TRADEMARK—MARCA REGISTRADA

Printed in the United States of America

Without limiting the rights under copyright reserved above, no part of this publication may be reproduced, stored in or introduced into a retrieval system, or transmitted, in any form, or by any means (electronic, mechanical, photocopying, recording, or otherwise), without the prior written permission of both the copyright owner and the above publisher of this book.

If you purchased this book without a cover you should be aware that this book is stolen property. It was reported as "unsold and destroyed" to the publisher and neither the author nor the publisher has received any payment for this "stripped book."

The scanning, uploading, and distribution of this book via the Internet or via any other means without the permission of the publisher is illegal and punishable by law. Please purchase only authorized electronic editions, and do not participate in or encourage electronic piracy of copyrighted materials. Your support of the author's rights is appreciated.

For Brian and Blake

Contents

INTRODUCTION
ix

BEOWULF
1

GLOSSARY OF NAMES
129

GENEALOGIES
139

AFTERWORD
141

Introduction

No one knows when *Beowulf* was composed, or by whom, or why. A single manuscript managed to survive Henry VIII's dissolution of the monasteries, and the destruction of their great libraries; since his name is written on one of the folios, Lawrence Nowell, the sixteenth-century scholar, may have been responsible for *Beowulf*'s preservation. The manuscript is a copy, in two distinct handwritings: how many other copies existed, or how close to the original this particular version was, will probably never be known. Indeed, since careless binding, plus an unfortunate fire in 1731, led in the course of time to serious deterioration of the manuscript, some words in *Beowulf* are known only from two transcripts made, in 1786–1787, by the Danish scholar Thorkelin. Other words, and lines, had either crumbled away before Thorkelin saw the manuscript, or are simply missing, or are incomplete; gaps have to be filled in by guesswork—and sometimes by ultraviolet photography.

But we do have the poem, and we are remarkably lucky to have it: not only is it unique, the sole survivor of what may have been a thriving epic tradition, but it is great poetry. Approached as an archaeological relic, it is fascinating. Taken as a linguistic document, it is a marvel, a mine of revelations and controversies. It gives us vital information about Old English social life and about Old English politics and about many things that scholars would like to have much more information on. But *Beowulf*'s position as a great poem must remain primary; the other purposes it serves are important but peripheral to this central fact of sheer literary merit.

It is essentially an aristocratic poem, concerned with kings and kingship:

> . . . He ruled
> Lands on all sides: wherever the sea
> Would take them his soldiers sailed, returned
> With tribute and obedience. There was a brave
> King!
>
> (8–12)

Strength and courage are basic virtues for both followed and follower. But where the follower's overriding commitment is to loyalty, the king's position is more complex.

> . . . A king
> Born, entrusted with ancient treasures
> And cities full of stronghearted soldiers,
> His vanity swelled him so vile and rank
> That he could hear no voices but his own. He deserved
> To suffer and die. . . .
>
> (908–913)

Thus Hermod is described, a king indisputably brave, incontestably strong, but unable to balance the requirements of absolute obedience with generosity and concern for his people's welfare, unable to simultaneously lead and sustain his soldiers. The poet immediately contrasts this savage brute, who would descend to drunken rages and kill his closest companions, with Beowulf, "a prince well-loved, followed in friendship, not fear."

The poem was composed in England perhaps four centuries before the Norman Conquest. And this England of roughly the eighth century A.D., as reflected in

Introduction

social patterns ascribed to sixth-century Geats and Danes and Swedes, is rigidly feudal, highly civilized and highly violent, and rather newly Christian. Layers of morality and tenderness and piety are intermixed, in *Beowulf,* with the glorification of war, death, and fame; such humdrum occupations as farming, fishing (except for sport: see lines 1432–1441), and the care and feeding of both adults and children are all denigrated, casually, when they are mentioned at all. Slavery is taken for granted: when a slave accompanies Beowulf and his men to the dragon's wasteland den, the poet does not include him in the count. There were *twelfa sum,* Beowulf and eleven others, we are told in line 2401, but five lines further on the poet adds that a *þreotteoð a secg,* a "thirteenth man"—the slave—was also with them. The important tools, in this poem, are weapons: proven swords and helmets are handed down, from father to son, like the vital treasures they were. Swords have personalities, and names; servants of course have neither.

Much of the poem is ruminative rather than, as might be expected, more narrowly narrative. Beowulf's three combats, with Grendel, Grendel's mother, and the dragon, occupy a surprisingly small part of the epic. As in the ceremonial wrestling of Japan, preliminaries—speeches, advice, reminiscences—are fully as important as actual fighting, and take longer in the telling. The poet can capture a battle scene with magnificent skill and vividness:

> Then the monster charged again, vomiting
> Fire, wild with pain, rushed out
> Fierce and dreadful, its fear forgotten.
> Watching for its chance it drove its tusks
> Into Beowulf's neck; he staggered, the blood
> Came flooding forth, fell like rain.
>
> (2688–2693)

And there can be no question of the relish with which

warfare is contemplated, its dominant role in this masculine-dominated society:

> ... No female, no matter
> How fierce, could have come with a man's strength,
> Fought with the power and courage men fight with,
> Smashing their shining swords, their bloody,
> Hammer-forged blades onto boar-headed helmets,
> Slashing and stabbing with the sharpest of points.
> (1282–1287)

But the significance of battle, rather than its bare facts, is what grips the poet. He is interested in what makes a good fighter tick, what makes a hero heroic; he looks inside the minds of both good men and evil monsters:

> ... Grendel
> Saw that his strength was deserting him, his claws
> Bound fast, Higlac's brave follower tearing at
> His hands. The monster's hatred rose higher,
> But his power had gone. He twisted in pain ...
> (811–815)

When Beowulf takes up the sword, "hammered by giants," which will give him victory over Grendel's mother, the poet's description is basically an internalized one—though the action is not neglected:

> ... savage, now, angry
> And desperate, [he] lifted it high over his head
> And struck with all the strength he had left ...
> (1563–1565)

It is God who grants Beowulf victory, but only after he is "back on his feet and fighting." The good fighter, the hero, the man who wins that most precious of all treasures, fame, is the man who never gives up, and who does not worry about the possible consequences of bravery:

> ... So fame
> Comes to the men who mean to win it
> And care about nothing else! ...
> (1534–1536)

Nor does it ever leave the hero, this driving will for glory:

> ... I am old, now,
> But I will fight again, seek fame still ...
> (2512–2513)

> ... But the brave old Swede
> Felt no fear: he quickly returned
> A better blow than he'd gotten, faced
> Toward Wulf and struck him savagely....
> (2967–2970)

Perhaps the most striking example of the perspective from which the poet sees battle, the context of values into which he constantly tries to fit it, is the climax of the fight with the dragon. Beowulf, weakened by time and age, is being slowly but surely beaten—"a king, before, but now a beaten warrior." His other comrades desert him, but Wiglaf stands watching, torn with indecision. About ten lines are given to his doubts (and his lineage). Then:

> ... Wiglaf's
> Mind was made up; he raised his yellow
> Shield and drew his sword ...
> (2608–2610)

Beowulf is in agony, "wrapped around in swirling flames," and the decision to go to his aid has been taken; the sword is drawn, the shield raised, and what follows? A lunge at the dragon, a scene of desperate combat? Not at all. The poet stops (by our standards) in midstream, gives us first twenty lines about Wiglaf's sword and how his father won it in battle, then another thirty lines of reproach for the cowards who had deserted their king in his time of need, and then, only then, resumes the action. At that, Wiglaf manages to make a final eight-line speech of encouragement as he goes diving "through the dragon's deadly fumes," running to Beowulf's side. The battle scene, tripartite now, is well worth waiting for; the point is that for the poet no battle is simply men hacking at each other (or at monsters of various descriptions). Battle is a way of life, a necessary function of the worthiest members of society. Kings, and warriors generally (samurai), are the successful men of the time, the corporation presidents, the space explorers, and the movie stars. They are people to be known about, to be emulated, but not blindly, not only because they are successful (death being the supreme product of their occupation). Theirs is the good and the true path; in their words, their thoughts, and their deeds they are the embodiment of the Anglo-Saxon way of life.

This morality, born of its time and its circumstances exactly as our belief in elections and multiple (and opposing) philosophies of government is born of our time and our circumstances, does not sound particularly Christian. And yet the poem is full of Christian sentiments, joined with or superimposed onto this more or less pagan code of battle-heroism-kingship (shared with the Danes and the Swedes and peoples all across Europe). Early students of *Beowulf* sometimes doubted that a single hand had composed the poem, much as early students of Homer doubted that "Homer" had ever existed, as a single human brain in a single human body. It seems fairly clear, however—and I myself have no doubt—that *Beowulf* is the work of one man and that its author was a Christian.

> ... the poet's clear songs, sung
> Of the ancient beginnings of us all, recalling
> The Almighty making the earth, shaping
> These beautiful plains marked off by oceans,
> Then proudly setting the sun and moon
> To glow across the land and light it;
> The corners of the earth were made lovely with trees
> And leaves, made quick with life, with each
> Of the nations who now move on its face....
>
> (90–98)

This so-called "Song of Creation," moving and eloquent as it is, enters the poem somewhat abruptly, following immediately on the introduction of Grendel, who is "living down in the darkness" and displeased that the Danes are happy in Herot, their new battle hall. Whoever wrote it was plainly a Christian, but we might say, having this before us and nothing more, that some monkish hand could have added these sentiments to improve and correct an essentially pagan epic. But most of the Christianity in *Beowulf* is not so easily dismissed as interpolation. "Let God be thanked!" (*Alwealdan þanc*), cries Hrothgar, for example, when the Danes assemble to celebrate Beowulf's victory over Grendel. These are his first words; he goes on, almost at once, to assert with great feeling that

> ... the Almighty makes miracles
> When He pleases, wonder after wonder, and this world
> Rests in His hands....
>
> (930–932)

It is God, as I have already noted, who leads Beowulf to victory over Grendel's vicious mother, once Beowulf has proved that he is willing and able to help himself. The examples could be multiplied many times over: the essential nature of this Christianity may not be quite the same as that practiced in twentieth-century London or in California, but it is an integral part of the poet's thought and of his view of life.

The "Song of Creation" shows, too, another of the poet's many gifts: his descriptive genius. None of his descriptive passages are autotelic; they are all purposeful, meant to elucidate or set the stage or accomplish a transition.

> And sometimes, when the path ran straight and clear,
> They would let their horses race, red
> And brown and pale yellow backs streaming
> Down the road. . . .
>
> (864–867)

This is intended, I think, to be a "true" picture rather than a "beautiful" one. The racing of horses was a proper and highly regarded sport; the animals were likely to be of these particular colors; and someone standing nearby and watching could easily see how accurate a description this was. The poet's listeners—like most Old English verse, *Beowulf* was meant to be heard rather than read—had undoubtedly seen such races themselves, many times over, and they would nod their heads in recognition and approval. This was indeed how it was—or how it should have been. But for us, to whom kings are unimportant and monsters nonexistent, to whom horses are objects to bet on and roads created for hundred-horsepower motors, what comes through most forcefully is quite simply the clear, sharp beauty of the scene.

The descriptions of imaginary events are just as vivid:

> They could see the water crawling with snakes,
> Fantastic serpents swimming in the boiling
> Lake, and sea beasts lying on the rocks
> —The kind that infest the ocean, in the early
> Dawn, often ending some ship's
> Journey with their wild jaws. . . .
>
> (1425–1430)

Introduction xvii

The poet had never seen anything like this lake of monsters; neither had his audience. It was vivid to them, I am confident, not as an exercise in imagery but as a conjuring up of what must exist, somewhere, somehow.

> There in the harbor was a ring-prowed fighting
> Ship, its timbers icy, waiting,
> And there they brought the belovèd body
> Of their ring-giving lord, and laid him near
> The mast. Next to that noble corpse
> They heaped up treasures, jeweled helmets,
> Hooked swords and coats of mail, armor
> Carried from the ends of the earth . . .
>
> (32–39)

The excavation of Sutton Hoo, a ceremonial and probably a kingly burial ship of perhaps the seventh century A.D., has shown how small a role fancy played in such descriptions. (The riches and wonders of Sutton Hoo need no cataloguing, here.) Like all poets, this one is capable of exaggeration, of stretching a point to make the story move more easily—but not in truly important matters, and the burial of a king was, for him, of an importance second to nothing. Even his talk of precious objects "carried from the ends of the earth" has been proven not a bit exaggerated: the Sutton Hoo burial treasures include a large silver dish stamped with the mark of the Byzantine Emperor Anastasius, who died in A.D. 518.

Almost most attractive to us, of all the many-sided excellences of *Beowulf,* is the poet's insight into people. Combining, in a sense, his concern for Anglo-Saxon morality with his descriptive and narrative powers, his delineation of men like Hrothgar and Wiglaf, the care and the eloquence of his portrayals, is deeply satisfying. Much of it is indirect, accomplished (like the best of contemporary fictional characterization) through his people's own words and movements. The eager excitement of Wulfgar, for example, hurrying off to announce Beowulf's arrival to King Hrothgar, fairly leaps from his five-line speech:

> Our warmhearted lord will be told
> Of your coming; I shall tell our king, our giver
> Of bright rings, and hurry back with his word,
> And speak it here, however he answers
> Your request. . . .
>
> (351–355)

Wulfgar's enthusiasm is all the more remarkable when we realize that visitors to a foreign king's court were usually beggars, outcasts, men whose feudal lord had died, rebels, or the like. That it could be dangerous, too, to welcome such men is shown by King Herdred's fate: see lines 2380–2390.

I have commented, in my *Poems from the Old English,* on the gentleness and solicitude shown by Wiglaf. The most notable characterization in the poem, I believe, is that of Hrothgar, who is brought to life with a fullness and subtlety to which no amount of quotation can do justice. But lesser figures are evoked with much the same skill. Hrothgar's queen, Welthow, is masterfully done: the irony of her appeals, on behalf of her young sons, must have been apparent to all who listened. Addressing her husband, and Hrothulf, his nephew, she says:

> . . . But your sons will be safe,
> Sheltered in Hrothulf's gracious protection,
> If fate takes their father while Hrothulf is alive;
> I know your nephew's kindness, I know
> He'll repay in kind the goodness you have shown him . . .
>
> (1180–1184)

Her view of the passion-filled Danish court, destined to erupt in treachery and murder after Hrothgar's death,

Introduction

includes such expressions of mistaken (or desperate?) good faith as this:

> All men speak softly, here, speak mildly
> And trust their neighbors, protect their lord,
> Are loyal followers who would fight as joyfully
> As they drink. . . .
>
> (1228–1231)

Her helplessness is pathetically plain.

Characters whose appearance is little more than incidental are also handled with perception and care: even the slave who stumbles onto the dragon, and who is later forced to lead Beowulf and his men to the monster, is "afraid of both beast and men." The nameless Geats, Beowulf's companions on his dangerous journey to Denmark, lie in the darkness of Herot, awaiting Grendel,

> . . . each of them sure that he was lost
> To the home he loved, to the high-walled towns
> And the friends he had left behind where both he
> And they had been raised. Each thought of the Danes
> Murdered by Grendel in a hall where Geats
> And not Danes now slept. . . .
>
> (691–696)

Some of the more or less self-contained episodes, like the famous Finn section (1068–1159), are developed with a tight, concise skill that shows the poet at ease in small forms as well as large. (Apparent obscurities in the Finn section, and elsewhere, are more our fault than his: too many centuries separate us, and too many universal allusions have become blank spaces for scholarship to struggle to fill.) The elegy of the last survivor of some unnamed noble race, lines 2247–2266, is worthy of comparison with such famous Old English poems as "The Ruin" and "Deor" (see, again, *Poems from the*

Old English). Indeed, though I have no evidence whatever, such is the poet's power and virtuosity that I do not believe it possible for *Beowulf* to have been the beginning and end of his literary production. His other work, both early and late, may well have been destroyed, along with all the rest of what must be missing from Old English literature. But it may not have been destroyed; some new Vercelli Book of precious and unique poetry may someday turn up, in an Italian monastery or almost anywhere else.

A few things should be said about this translation, its sources, principles, and practice. My basic text has been F. Klaeber's *Beowulf* (3rd edition, with 1st and 2nd supplements, 1950). I have also made extensive use of E. V. K. Dobbie's *Beowulf,* in the indispensable Anglo-Saxon Poetic Records series (vol. IV, 1953). A few disputed readings of the manuscript have been drawn from C. L. Wrenn's *Beowulf* (1953). Other works consulted with some frequency include Bosworth/Toller, *An Anglo-Saxon Dictionary* (1898); Toller's *Supplement* (1921); J. R. Clark Hall, *A Concise Anglo-Saxon Dictionary* (4th edition, with a supplement by H. D. Meritt, 1960); A. J. Wyatt, *An Anglo-Saxon Reader* (1919); R. Quirk and C. L. Wrenn, *An Old English Grammar* (2nd edition, 1958); and J. and E. M. Wright, *Old English Grammar* (3rd edition, 1925). I have also consulted David Wright's prose translation, *Beowulf* (1957), and the R. K. Gordon prose translation, in his *Anglo-Saxon Poetry* (1954). And I commend, to the interested and zealous reader, R. W. Chambers, *Beowulf* (3rd edition, with a supplement by C. L. Wrenn, 1959), and two excellent little books by Dorothy Whitelock, *The Audience of Beowulf* (1951) and *The Beginnings of English Society* (1952).

If this listing of authorities makes the translation of *Beowulf* seem like a task weighted with scholarly apparatus (and implications), I can only admit that anyone working with a text so complex and, still, so imperfectly understood, must necessarily rely heavily on every authority he can lay his hands on. It may well be sufficient, at this point, to cite roughly *one-half* of Dobbie's note on the single word *higemæðum,* which occurs in line 2909:

> This word has been variously explained, by some as dat. plur. of a noun, by others as dat. plur. of an adjective. Thorpe read *hige meðum* as two words, "with weary spirit"; all other edd. print as a compound. Sievers, *Beitr.* IX, 142 f., suggested emending to *higemeðe,* adjective, "weary of mind," referring to Wiglaf; this emendation was adopted by Holder (1 ed.), Holthausen (1, 2 ed.), and Sedgefield (1 ed.), but was later withdrawn by Sievers in *Beitr.* XXXVI, 419. Grein, *Spr.* II, 128, assumed a noun *higemæðu,* which he doubtfully glossed as "reverentia, diligentia"; Grein, ed., identified the second element of the compound with *mæð,* "measure," and translated *higemæð* (p. 139) as "geziemende Gesinnung, aufmerksame Sorgfalt." A noun *higemæð,* "reverence," is accepted by Wyatt (who glosses it as "mind-honour, heart-reverence"), Schücking, and Chambers. Sedgefield (3 ed.), note, translates, " 'with balance of mind,' *i.e.* impartially"; see also his note in *MLRev.* XXVIII, 229. Rieger, *ZfdPh.* III, 413, would read *higemeðum,* dat. plur. of the adjective, referring to both the dead Beowulf and the dragon; so Heyne (4 ed.) and Socin.... For a more complete account of the scholarship on this word, see Hoops, *Bwst.*, pp. 137 f.

This is not in the least atypical; if it does not inspire awe, it should at least create a feeling of sympathy.

My personal credo, with regard to the making of translations, has not changed since *Poems from the Old*

English: the following comments from pages xxvi and xxix of that book are still applicable, here.

> The translator's only hope is to re-create something roughly equivalent in the new language, something that is itself good poetry and that at the same time carries a reasonable measure of the force and flavor of the original. In this sense a re-creation can only be a creation. . . . Comparatively few lines would meet a *scop*'s exacting standards. Essentially, I have used a free four-beat line, without regard to the usual accent patterns of English verse: the translations are therefore not tetrameter, in the usual sense of iamb or trochee.

My practice has, however, varied somewhat, and particularly in the matter of alliteration. *Beowulf* is a poem of 3,182 lines; techniques adequate to a group of shorter works will not necessarily serve it equally well. I have felt it advisable, even obligatory, to alliterate much more freely, occasionally as the Old English alliterates, more usually in irregular patterns developed *ad hoc*. These patterns include everything from alliteration on the first and fourth stresses to alliteration that runs through and across several lines. I have also used part-alliteration; I have sometimes used paired alliteration—two words in a line alliterating according to one sound, and the other two alliterating according to a wholly different sound; I have even, though infrequently and, I hope, most discreetly, used a bit of internal rhyme. I should perhaps add that I have tried to let the weight and motion of each line determine where the stresses (four to a line) fall. The same word, therefore, need not be an alliterating word (i.e., a stressed word) each time it occurs.

Finally, I want to thank Professor Angel Flores, who commissioned a section of this translation and so got me started on a task the size of which had always frightened me away; Professor Robert P. Creed, who gave me most welcome encouragement, and who not only cheerfully but actually eagerly read through the entire manuscript, making many helpful suggestions en route; Professor J. B. Bessinger, of whom—though it seems almost incredible that a translator should have *two* such selfless readers—the same must be said; and my two oldest sons, Brian and Blake, who bore with my preoccupation, who looked bright-eyed and interested when I retold the story for them, blow by blow, and who (age nine and age eight) promised to sit and read proof with me—and (age ten and age nine) did.

—Burton Raffel

BEOWULF

Prologue

Hear me! We've heard of Danish heroes,
Ancient kings and the glory they cut
For themselves, swinging mighty swords!
How Shild made slaves of soldiers from every
Land, crowds of captives he'd beaten
Into terror; he'd traveled to Denmark alone,
An abandoned child, but changed his own fate,
Lived to be rich and much honored. He ruled
Lands on all sides: wherever the sea
Would take them his soldiers sailed, returned
With tribute and obedience. There was a brave
King! And he gave them more than his glory,
Conceived a son for the Danes, a new leader
Allowed them by the grace of God. They had lived,
Before his coming, kingless and miserable;
Now the Lord of all life, Ruler
Of glory, blessed them with a prince, Beo,
Whose power and fame soon spread through the world.
Shild's strong son was the glory of Denmark;
His father's warriors were wound round his heart
With golden rings, bound to their prince
By his father's treasure. So young men build
The future, wisely open-handed in peace,
Protected in war; so warriors earn
Their fame, and wealth is shaped with a sword.

Beowulf

When his time was come the old king died,
Still strong but called to the Lord's hands.
His comrades carried him down to the shore,
Bore him as their leader had asked, their lord
And companion, while words could move on his tongue.
30 Shild's reign had been long; he'd ruled them well.
There in the harbor was a ring-prowed fighting
Ship, its timbers icy, waiting,
And there they brought the belovèd body
35 Of their ring-giving lord, and laid him near
The mast. Next to that noble corpse
They heaped up treasures, jeweled helmets,
Hooked swords and coats of mail, armor
Carried from the ends of the earth: no ship
40 Had ever sailed so brightly fitted,
No king sent forth more deeply mourned.
Forced to set him adrift, floating
As far as the tide might run, they refused
To give him less from their hoards of gold
45 Than those who'd shipped him away, an orphan
And a beggar, to cross the waves alone.
High up over his head they flew
His shining banner, then sadly let
The water pull at the ship, watched it
50 Slowly sliding to where neither rulers
Nor heroes nor anyone can say whose hands
Opened to take that motionless cargo.

1

Then Beo was king in that Danish castle,
Shild's son ruling as long as his father
And as loved, a famous lord of men.
And he in turn gave his people a son,
The great Healfdane, a fierce fighter
Who led the Danes to the end of his long
Life and left them four children,
Three princes to guide them in battle, Hergar
And Hrothgar and Halga the Good, and one daughter,
Yrs, who was given to Onela, king
Of the Swedes, and became his wife and their queen.
  Then Hrothgar, taking the throne, led
The Danes to such glory that comrades and kinsmen
Swore by his sword, and young men swelled
His armies, and he thought of greatness and resolved
To build a hall that would hold his mighty
Band and reach higher toward Heaven than anything
That had ever been known to the sons of men.
And in that hall he'd divide the spoils
Of their victories, to old and young what they'd earned
In battle, but leaving the common pastures
Untouched, and taking no lives. The work
Was ordered, the timbers tied and shaped

By the hosts that Hrothgar ruled. It was quickly
Ready, that most beautiful of dwellings, built
As he'd wanted, and then he whose word was obeyed
All over the earth named it Herot.

80 His boast come true he commanded a banquet,
Opened out his treasure-full hands.
That towering place, gabled and huge,
Stood waiting for time to pass, for war
To begin, for flames to leap as high
As the feud that would light them, and for Herot to burn.

85 A powerful monster, living down
In the darkness, growled in pain, impatient
As day after day the music rang
Loud in that hall, the harp's rejoicing
90 Call and the poet's clear songs, sung
Of the ancient beginnings of us all, recalling
The Almighty making the earth, shaping
These beautiful plains marked off by oceans,
Then proudly setting the sun and moon
95 To glow across the land and light it;
The corners of the earth were made lovely with trees
And leaves, made quick with life, with each
Of the nations who now move on its face. And then
As now warriors sang of their pleasure:
100 So Hrothgar's men lived happy in his hall
Till the monster stirred, that demon, that fiend,
Grendel, who haunted the moors, the wild
Marshes, and made his home in a hell
Not hell but earth. He was spawned in that slime,
105 Conceived by a pair of those monsters born
Of Cain, murderous creatures banished
By God, punished forever for the crime
Of Abel's death. The Almighty drove
Those demons out, and their exile was bitter,
110 Shut away from men; they split

Into a thousand forms of evil—spirits
And fiends, goblins, monsters, giants,
A brood forever opposing the Lord's
Will, and again and again defeated.

} Pagan?

2

¹¹⁵ Then, when darkness had dropped, Grendel
Went up to Herot, wondering what the warriors
Would do in that hall when their drinking was done.
He found them sprawled in sleep, suspecting
Nothing, their dreams undisturbed. The monster's
¹²⁰ Thoughts were as quick as his greed or his claws:
He slipped through the door and there in the silence
Snatched up thirty men, smashed them
Unknowing in their beds and ran out with their bodies,
The blood dripping behind him, back
¹²⁵ To his lair, delighted with his night's slaughter.
   At daybreak, with the sun's first light, they saw
How well he had worked, and in that gray morning
Broke their long feast with tears and laments
For the dead. Hrothgar, their lord, sat joyless
¹³⁰ In Herot, a mighty prince mourning
The fate of his lost friends and companions,
Knowing by its tracks that some demon had torn
His followers apart. He wept, fearing
The beginning might not be the end. And that night
¹³⁵ Grendel came again, so set
On murder that no crime could ever be enough,
No savage assault quench his lust
For evil. Then each warrior tried

Beowulf

To escape him, searched for rest in different
Beds, as far from Herot as they could find, 140
Seeing how Grendel hunted when they slept.
Distance was safety; the only survivors
Were those who fled him. Hate had triumphed.

  So Grendel ruled, fought with the righteous,
One against many, and won; so Herot 145
Stood empty, and stayed deserted for years,
Twelve winters of grief for Hrothgar, king
Of the Danes, sorrow heaped at his door
By hell-forged hands. His misery leaped
The seas, was told and sung in all 150
Men's ears: how Grendel's hatred began,
How the monster relished his savage war
On the Danes, keeping the bloody feud
Alive, seeking no peace, offering
No truce, accepting no settlement, no price 155
In gold or land, and paying the living
For one crime only with another. No one
Waited for reparation from his plundering claws:
That shadow of death hunted in the darkness,
Stalked Hrothgar's warriors, old 160
And young, lying in waiting, hidden
In mist, invisibly following them from the edge
Of the marsh, always there, unseen.

  So mankind's enemy continued his crimes,
Killing as often as he could, coming 165
Alone, bloodthirsty and horrible. Though he lived
In Herot, when the night hid him, he never
Dared to touch king Hrothgar's glorious
Throne, protected by God—God,
Whose love Grendel could not know. But Hrothgar's 170
Heart was bent. The best and most noble
Of his council debated remedies, sat
In secret sessions, talking of terror
And wondering what the bravest of warriors
    could do.
And sometimes they sacrificed to the old stone gods, 175

Made heathen vows, hoping for Hell's
Support, the Devil's guidance in driving
Their affliction off. That was their way,
And the heathen's only hope, Hell
180 Always in their hearts, knowing neither God
Nor His passing as He walks through our world, the Lord
Of Heaven and earth; their ears could not hear
His praise nor know His glory. Let them
Beware, those who are thrust into danger,
185 Clutched at by trouble, yet can carry no solace
In their hearts, cannot hope to be better! Hail
To those who will rise to God, drop off
Their dead bodies and seek our Father's peace!

3

So the living sorrow of Healfdane's son
Simmered, bitter and fresh, and no wisdom *190*
Or strength could break it: that agony hung
On king and people alike, harsh
And unending, violent and cruel, and evil.
  In his far-off home Beowulf, Higlac's
Follower and the strongest of the Geats—greater *195*
And stronger than anyone anywhere in this world—
Heard how Grendel filled nights with horror
And quickly commanded a boat fitted out,
Proclaiming that he'd go to that famous king,
Would sail across the sea to Hrothgar, *200*
Now when help was needed. None
Of the wise ones regretted his going, much
As he was loved by the Geats: the omens were
     good,
And they urged the adventure on. So Beowulf
Chose the mightiest men he could find, *205*
The bravest and best of the Geats, fourteen
In all, and led them down to their boat;
He knew the sea, would point the prow
Straight to that distant Danish shore.
  Then they sailed, set their ship *210*
Out on the waves, under the cliffs.
Ready for what came they wound through the
     currents,

The seas beating at the sand, and were borne
In the lap of their shining ship, lined [Alliteration]
With gleaming armor, going safely
In that oak-hard boat to where their hearts took
   them.
The wind hurried them over the waves, [Simile]
The ship foamed through the sea like a bird
Until, in the time they had known it would take,
Standing in the round-curled prow they could see
Sparkling hills, high and green,
Jutting up over the shore, and rejoicing
In those rock-steep cliffs they quietly ended
Their voyage. Jumping to the ground, the Geats
Pushed their boat to the sand and tied it
In place, mail shirts and armor rattling
As they swiftly moored their ship. And then
They gave thanks to God for their easy crossing.
   High on a wall a Danish watcher
Patrolling along the cliffs saw
The travelers crossing to the shore, their shields
Raised and shining; he came riding down,
Hrothgar's lieutenant, spurring his horse,
Needing to know why they'd landed, these men
In armor. Shaking his heavy spear
In their faces he spoke:
                     "Whose soldiers are you,
You who've been carried in your deep-keeled ship
Across the sea-road to this country of mine?
Listen! I've stood on these cliffs longer
Than you know, keeping our coast free
Of pirates, raiders sneaking ashore
From their ships, seeking our lives and our gold.
None have ever come more openly—
And yet you've offered no password, no sign
From my prince, no permission from my people for
   your landing
Here. Nor have I ever seen,
Out of all the men on earth, one greater

Than has come with you; no commoner carries
Such weapons, unless his appearance, and his beauty, 250
Are both lies. You! Tell me your name,
And your father's; no spies go further onto Danish
Soil than you've come already. Strangers,
From wherever it was you sailed, tell it,
And tell it quickly, the quicker the better, 255
I say, for us all. Speak, say
Exactly who you are, and from where, and why."

4

Their leader answered him, Beowulf unlocking
Words from deep in his breast:
                              "We are Geats,
Men who follow Higlac. My father
Was a famous soldier, known far and wide
As a leader of men. His name was Edgetho.
His life lasted many winters;
Wise men all over the earth surely
Remember him still. And we have come seeking
Your prince, Healfdane's son, protector
Of this people, only in friendship: instruct us,
Watchman, help us with your words! Our errand
Is a great one, our business with the glorious king
Of the Danes no secret; there's nothing dark
Or hidden in our coming. You know (if we've heard
The truth, and been told honestly) that your country
Is cursed with some strange, vicious creature
That hunts only at night and that no one
Has seen. It's said, watchman, that he has slaughtered
Your people, brought terror to the darkness. Perhaps
Hrothgar can hunt, here in my heart,
For some way to drive this devil out—

Beowulf

If anything will ever end the evils 280
Afflicting your wise and famous lord.
Here he can cool his burning sorrow.
Or else he may see his suffering go on
Forever, for as long as Herot towers
High on your hills." 285
              The mounted officer
Answered him bluntly, the brave watchman:
"A soldier should know the difference between
   words
And deeds, and keep that knowledge clear
In his brain. I believe your words, I trust in 290
Your friendship. Go forward, weapons and armor
And all, on into Denmark. I'll guide you
Myself—and my men will guard your ship,
Keep it safe here on our shores,
Your fresh-tarred boat, watch it well, 295
Until that curving prow carries
Across the sea to Geatland a chosen
Warrior who bravely does battle with the creature
Haunting our people, who survives that horror
Unhurt, and goes home bearing our love." 300
   Then they moved on. Their boat lay moored,
Tied tight to its anchor. Glittering at the top
Of their golden helmets wild boar heads gleamed,
Shining decorations, swinging as they marched,
Erect like guards, like sentinels, as though ready 305
To fight. They marched, Beowulf and his men
And their guide, until they could see the gables
Of Herot, covered with hammered gold
And glowing in the sun—that most famous of all
   dwellings,
Towering majestic, its glittering roofs 310
Visible far across the land.
Their guide reined in his horse, pointing
To that hall, built by Hrothgar for the best
And bravest of his men; the path was plain,
They could see their way. And then he spoke: 315

"Now I must leave you: may the Lord our God
Protect your coming and going! The sea
Is my job, keeping these coasts free
Of invaders, bands of pirates: I must go back."

5

The path he'd shown them was paved, cobbled 320
Like a Roman road. They arrived with their mail
   shirts
Glittering, silver-shining links
Clanking an iron song as they came.
Sea-weary still, they set their broad,
Battle-hardened shields in rows 325
Along the wall, then stretched themselves
On Herot's benches. Their armor rang;
Their ash-wood spears stood in a line,
Gray-tipped and straight: the Geats' war-gear
Were honored weapons. 330
                        A Danish warrior
Asked who they were, their names and their
   fathers':
  "Where have you carried these gold-carved
     shields from,
These silvery shirts and helmets, and those spears
Set out in long lines? I am Hrothgar's 335
Herald and captain. Strangers have come here
Before, but never so freely, so bold.
And you come too proudly to be exiles: not poverty
But your hearts' high courage has brought you to
   Hrothgar."
  He was answered by a famous soldier, the Geats' 340
Proud prince:

17

"We follow Higlac, break bread
At his side. I am Beowulf. My errand
Is for Healfdane's great son to hear, your glorious
345 Lord; if he chooses to receive us we will greet him,
Salute the chief of the Danes and speak out
Our message."
       Wulfgar replied—a prince
Born to the Swedes, famous for both strength
350 And wisdom:
       "Our warmhearted lord will be told
Of your coming; I shall tell our king, our giver
Of bright rings, and hurry back with his word,
And speak it here, however he answers
355 Your request."
       He went quickly to where Hrothgar sat,
Gray and old, in the middle of his men,
And knowing the custom of that court walked straight
To the king's great chair, stood waiting to be heard,
360 Then spoke:
       "There are Geats who have come sailing the open
Ocean to our land, come far over
The high waves, led by a warrior
Called Beowulf. They wait on your word, bring messages
365 For your ears alone. My lord, grant them
A gracious answer, see them and hear
What they've come for! Their weapons and armor are nobly
Worked—these men are no beggars. And Beowulf
Their prince, who showed them the way to our shores,
370 Is a mighty warrior, powerful and wise."

6

The Danes' high prince and protector answered:
"I knew Beowulf as a boy. His father
Was Edgetho, who was given Hrethel's one daughter
—Hrethel, Higlac's father. Now Edgetho's
Brave son is here, come visiting a friendly 375
King. And I've heard that when seamen came,
Bringing their gifts and presents to the Geats,
They wrestled and ran together, and Higlac's
Young prince showed them a mighty battle-grip,
Hands that moved with thirty men's strength, 380
And courage to match. Our Holy Father
Has sent him as a sign of His grace, a mark
Of His favor, to help us defeat Grendel
And end that terror. I shall greet him with treasures,
Gifts to reward his courage in coming to us. 385
Quickly, order them all to come to me
Together, Beowulf and his band of Geats.
And tell them, too, how welcome we will make them!"
  Then Wulfgar went to the door and addressed
The waiting seafarers with soldier's words: 390
  "My lord, the great king of the Danes, commands me
To tell you that he knows of your noble birth

Beowulf

And that having come to him from over the open
Sea you have come bravely and are welcome.
Now go to him as you are, in your armor and helmets,
But leave your battle-shields here, and your spears,
Let them lie waiting for the promises your words
May make."

               Beowulf arose, with his men
Around him, ordering a few to remain
With their weapons, leading the others quickly
Along under Herot's steep roof into Hrothgar's
Presence. Standing on that prince's own hearth,
Helmeted, the silvery metal of his mail shirt
Gleaming with a smith's high art, he greeted
The Danes' great lord:

               "Hail, Hrothgar!
Higlac is my cousin and my king; the days
Of my youth have been filled with glory. Now Grendel's
Name has echoed in our land: sailors
Have brought us stories of Herot, the best
Of all mead-halls, deserted and useless when the moon
Hangs in skies the sun had lit,
Light and life fleeing together.
My people have said, the wisest, most knowing
And best of them, that my duty was to go to the Danes'
Great king. They have seen my strength for themselves,
Have watched me rise from the darkness of war,
Dripping with my enemies' blood. I drove
Five great giants into chains, chased
All of that race from the earth. I swam
In the blackness of night, hunting monsters
Out of the ocean, and killing them one
By one; death was my errand and the fate
They had earned. Now Grendel and I are called

Together, and I've come. Grant me, then,
Lord and protector of this noble place,
A single request! I have come so far,
O shelterer of warriors and your people's loved
    friend,
That this one favor you should not refuse me—　430
That I, alone and with the help of my men,
May purge all evil from this hall. I have heard,
Too, that the monster's scorn of men
Is so great that he needs no weapons and fears
    none.
Nor will I. My lord Higlac　435
Might think less of me if I let my sword
Go where my feet were afraid to, if I hid
Behind some broad linden shield: my hands
Alone shall fight for me, struggle for life
Against the monster. God must decide　440
Who will be given to death's cold grip.
Grendel's plan, I think, will be
What it has been before, to invade this hall
And gorge his belly with our bodies. If he can,
If he can. And I think, if my time will have come,　445
There'll be nothing to mourn over, no corpse to
    prepare
For its grave: Grendel will carry our bloody
Flesh to the moors, crunch on our bones
And smear torn scraps of our skin on the walls
Of his den. No, I expect no Danes　450
Will fret about sewing our shrouds, if he wins.
And if death does take me, send the hammered
Mail of my armor to Higlac, return
The inheritance I had from Hrethel, and he
From Wayland. Fate will unwind as it must!"　455

7

Hrothgar replied, protector of the Danes:
"Beowulf, you've come to us in friendship, and because
Of the reception your father found at our court.
Edgetho had begun a bitter feud,
Killing Hathlaf, a Wulfing warrior:
Your father's countrymen were afraid of war,
If he returned to his home, and they turned him away.
Then he traveled across the curving waves
To the land of the Danes. I was new to the throne,
Then, a young man ruling this wide
Kingdom and its golden city: Hergar,
My older brother, a far better man
Than I, had died and dying made me,
Second among Healfdane's sons, first
In this nation. I bought the end of Edgetho's
Quarrel, sent ancient treasures through the ocean's
Furrows to the Wulfings; your father swore
He'd keep that peace. My tongue grows heavy,
And my heart, when I try to tell you what Grendel
Has brought us, the damage he's done, here
In this hall. You see for yourself how much smaller
Our ranks have become, and can guess what we've lost
To his terror. Surely the Lord Almighty
Could stop his madness, smother his lust!
How many times have my men, glowing
With courage drawn from too many cups

Of ale, sworn to stay after dark
And stem that horror with a sweep of their swords.
And then, in the morning, this mead-hall glittering
With new light would be drenched with blood, the
   benches   485
Stained red, the floors, all wet from that fiend's
Savage assault—and my soldiers would be fewer
Still, death taking more and more.
But to table, Beowulf, a banquet in your honor:
Let us toast your victories, and talk of the future."   490
   Then Hrothgar's men gave places to the Geats,
Yielded benches to the brave visitors
And led them to the feast. The keeper of the mead
Came carrying out the carved flasks,
And poured that bright sweetness. A poet   495
Sang, from time to time, in a clear
Pure voice. Danes and visiting Geats
Celebrated as one, drank and rejoiced.

8

Unferth spoke, Ecglaf's son,
Who sat at Hrothgar's feet, spoke harshly
And sharp (vexed by Beowulf's adventure,
By their visitor's courage, and angry that anyone
In Denmark or anywhere on earth had ever
Acquired glory and fame greater
Than his own):

"You're Beowulf, are you—the same
Boastful fool who fought a swimming
Match with Brecca, both of you daring
And young and proud, exploring the deepest
Seas, risking your lives for no reason
But the danger? All older and wiser heads warned
     you
Not to, but no one could check such pride.
With Brecca at your side you swam along
The sea-paths, your swift-moving hands pulling you
Over the ocean's face. Then winter
Churned through the water, the waves ran you
As they willed, and you struggled seven long nights
To survive. And at the end victory was his,
Not yours. The sea carried him close
To his home, to southern Norway, near
The land of the Brondings, where he ruled and
     was loved,

Beowulf

Where his treasure was piled and his strength protected
His towns and his people. He'd promised to outswim you:
Bonstan's son made that boast ring true.
You've been lucky in your battles, Beowulf, but I think 525
Your luck may change if you challenge Grendel,
Staying a whole night through in this hall,
Waiting where that fiercest of demons can find you."

Beowulf answered, Edgetho's great son:
"Ah! Unferth, my friend, your face 530
Is hot with ale, and your tongue has tried
To tell us about Brecca's doings. But the truth
Is simple: no man swims in the sea
As I can, no strength is a match for mine.
As boys, Brecca and I had boasted— 535
We were both too young to know better—that we'd risk
Our lives far out at sea, and so
We did. Each of us carried a naked
Sword, prepared for whales or the swift
Sharp teeth and beaks of needlefish. 540
He could never leave me behind, swim faster
Across the waves than I could, and I
Had chosen to remain close to his side.
I remained near him for five long nights,
Until a flood swept us apart; 545
The frozen sea surged around me,
It grew dark, the wind turned bitter, blowing
From the north, and the waves were savage. Creatures
Who sleep deep in the sea were stirred
Into life—and the iron hammered links 550
Of my mail shirt, these shining bits of metal
Woven across my breast, saved me
From death. A monster seized me, drew me

Swiftly toward the bottom, swimming with its claws
Tight in my flesh. But fate let me
Find its heart with my sword, hack myself
Free; I fought that beast's last battle,
Left it floating lifeless in the sea.

9

"Other monsters crowded around me,
Continually attacking. I treated them politely, 560
Offering the edge of my razor-sharp sword.
But the feast, I think, did not please them, filled
Their evil bellies with no banquet-rich food,
Thrashing there at the bottom of the sea;
By morning they'd decided to sleep on the shore, 565
Lying on their backs, their blood spilled out
On the sand. Afterwards, sailors could cross
That sea-road and feel no fear; nothing
Would stop their passing. Then God's bright beacon
Appeared in the east, the water lay still, 570
And at last I could see the land, wind-swept
Cliff-walls at the edge of the coast. Fate saves
The living when they drive away death by themselves!
Lucky or not, nine was the number
Of sea-huge monsters I killed. What man, 575
Anywhere under Heaven's high arch, has fought
In such darkness, endured more misery or been harder
Pressed? Yet I survived the sea, smashed
The monsters' hot jaws, swam home from my journey.
The swift-flowing waters swept me along 580
And I landed on Finnish soil. I've heard

No tales of you, Unferth, telling
Of such clashing terror, such contests in the night!
Brecca's battles were never so bold;
Neither he nor you can match me—and I mean
No boast, have announced no more than I know
To be true. And there's more: you murdered your brothers,
Your own close kin. Words and bright wit
Won't help your soul; you'll suffer hell's fires,
Unferth, forever tormented. Ecglaf's
Proud son, if your hands were as hard, your heart
As fierce as you think it, no fool would dare
To raid your hall, ruin Herot
And oppress its prince, as Grendel has done.
But he's learned that terror is his alone,
Discovered he can come for your people with no fear
Of reprisal; he's found no fighting, here,
But only food, only delight.
He murders as he likes, with no mercy, gorges
And feasts on your flesh, and expects no trouble,
No quarrel from the quiet Danes. Now
The Geats will show him courage, soon
He can test his strength in battle. And when the sun
Comes up again, opening another
Bright day from the south, anyone in Denmark
May enter this hall: that evil will be gone!"
  Hrothgar, gray-haired and brave, sat happily
Listening, the famous ring-giver sure,
At last, that Grendel could be killed; he believed
In Beowulf's bold strength and the firmness of his
    spirit.
    There was the sound of laughter, and the cheerful clanking
Of cups, and pleasant words. Then Welthow,
Hrothgar's gold-ringed queen, greeted
The warriors; a noble woman who knew
What was right, she raised a flowing cup

To Hrothgar first, holding it high
For the lord of the Danes to drink, wishing him
Joy in that feast. The famous king
Drank with pleasure and blessed their banquet.
Then Welthow went from warrior to warrior, 620
Pouring a portion from the jeweled cup
For each, till the bracelet-wearing queen
Had carried the mead-cup among them and it was
    Beowulf's
Turn to be served. She saluted the Geats'
Great prince, thanked God for answering her
    prayers, 625
For allowing her hands the happy duty
Of offering mead to a hero who would help
Her afflicted people. He drank what she poured,
Edgetho's brave son, then assured the Danish
Queen that his heart was firm and his hands 630
Ready:
        "When we crossed the sea, my comrades
And I, I already knew that all
My purpose was this: to win the goodwill
Of your people or die in battle, pressed 635
In Grendel's fierce grip. Let me live in greatness
And courage, or here in this hall welcome
My death!"
        Welthow was pleased with his words,
His bright-tongued boasts; she carried them back 640
To her lord, walked nobly across to his side.
   The feast went on, laughter and music
And the brave words of warriors celebrating
Their delight. Then Hrothgar rose, Healfdane's
Son, heavy with sleep; as soon 645
As the sun had gone, he knew that Grendel
Would come to Herot, would visit that hall
When night had covered the earth with its net
And the shapes of darkness moved black and silent
Through the world. Hrothgar's warriors rose with
    him. 650

He went to Beowulf, embraced the Geats'
Brave prince, wished him well, and hoped
That Herot would be his to command. And then
He declared:

655   "No one strange to this land
Has ever been granted what I've given you,
No one in all the years of my rule.
Make this best of all mead-halls yours, and then
Keep it free of evil, fight
660 With glory in your heart! Purge Herot
And your ship will sail home with its treasure-
    holds full."

1. What is the current setting?
2. Why does Beowulf say he fell behind in the swimming match?
3. What does Beowulf say Unferth did?
4. What characters are in this section?

10

Then Hrothgar left that hall, the Danes'
Great protector, followed by his court; the queen
Had preceded him and he went to lie at her side,
Seek sleep near his wife. It was said that God
Himself had set a sentinel in Herot,
Brought Beowulf as a guard against Grendel and
   a shield
Behind whom the king could safely rest.
And Beowulf was ready, firm with our Lord's
High favor and his own bold courage and strength.
   He stripped off his mail shirt, his helmet, his
      sword
Hammered from the hardest iron, and handed
All his weapons and armor to a servant,
Ordered his war-gear guarded till morning.
And then, standing beside his bed,
He exclaimed:—
         "Grendel is no braver, no stronger
Than I am! I could kill him with my sword; I shall
   not,
Easy as it would be. This fiend is a bold
And famous fighter, but his claws and teeth
Scratching at my shield, his clumsy fists
Beating at my sword blade, would be helpless. I will
   meet him
With my hands empty—unless his heart

Fails him, seeing a soldier waiting
685 Weaponless, unafraid. Let God in His wisdom
Extend His hand where He wills, reward
Whom He chooses!"
         Then the Geats' great chief dropped
His head to his pillow, and around him, as ready
As they could be, lay the soldiers who had crossed
690   the sea
At his side, each of them sure that he was lost
To the home he loved, to the high-walled towns
And the friends he had left behind where both he
And they had been raised. Each thought of the Danes
695 Murdered by Grendel in a hall where Geats
And not Danes now slept. But God's dread loom
Was woven with defeat for the monster, good fortune
For the Geats; help against Grendel was with them,
And through the might of a single man
They would win. Who doubts that God in His
700   wisdom
And strength holds the earth forever
In His hands? Out in the darkness the monster
Began to walk. The warriors slept
In that gabled hall where they hoped that He
705 Would keep them safe from evil, guard them
From death till the end of their days was determined
And the thread should be broken. But Beowulf lay wakeful,
Watching, waiting, eager to meet
His enemy, and angry at the thought of his coming.

11

   Out from the marsh, from the foot of misty   710
Hills and bogs, bearing God's hatred,
Grendel came, hoping to kill
Anyone he could trap on this trip to high Herot.
He moved quickly through the cloudy night,
Up from his swampland, sliding silently   715
Toward that gold-shining hall. He had visited Hrothgar's
Home before, knew the way—
But never, before nor after that night,
Found Herot defended so firmly, his reception
So harsh. He journeyed, forever joyless,   720
Straight to the door, then snapped it open,
Tore its iron fasteners with a touch
And rushed angrily over the threshold.
He strode quickly across the inlaid
Floor, snarling and fierce: his eyes   725
Gleamed in the darkness, burned with a gruesome
Light. Then he stopped, seeing the hall
Crowded with sleeping warriors, stuffed
With rows of young soldiers resting together.
And his heart laughed, he relished the sight,   730
Intended to tear the life from those bodies
By morning; the monster's mind was hot
With the thought of food and the feasting his belly
Would soon know. But fate, that night, intended

33

735 Grendel to gnaw the broken bones
Of his last human supper. Human
Eyes were watching his evil steps,
Waiting to see his swift hard claws.
Grendel snatched at the first Geat
740 He came to, ripped him apart, cut
His body to bits with powerful jaws,
Drank the blood from his veins and bolted
Him down, hands and feet; death
And Grendel's great teeth came together,
745 Snapping life shut. Then he stepped to another
Still body, clutched at Beowulf with his claws,
Grasped at a strong-hearted wakeful sleeper
—And was instantly seized himself, claws
Bent back as Beowulf leaned up on one arm.
750 That shepherd of evil, guardian of crime,
Knew at once that nowhere on earth
Had he met a man whose hands were harder;
His mind was flooded with fear—but nothing
Could take his talons and himself from that tight
755 Hard grip. Grendel's one thought was to run
From Beowulf, flee back to his marsh and hide there:
This was a different Herot than the hall he had emptied.
But Higlac's follower remembered his final
Boast and, standing erect, stopped
760 The monster's flight, fastened those claws
In his fists till they cracked, clutched Grendel
Closer. The infamous killer fought
For his freedom, wanting no flesh but retreat,
Desiring nothing but escape; his claws
Had been caught, he was trapped. That trip to Herot
765 Was a miserable journey for the writhing monster!
  The high hall rang, its roof boards swayed,
And Danes shook with terror. Down
The aisles the battle swept, angry

And wild. Herot trembled, wonderfully
Built to withstand the blows, the struggling
Great bodies beating at its beautiful walls;
Shaped and fastened with iron, inside
And out, artfully worked, the building
Stood firm. Its benches rattled, fell
To the floor, gold-covered boards grating
As Grendel and Beowulf battled across them.
Hrothgar's wise men had fashioned Herot
To stand forever; only fire,
They had planned, could shatter what such skill had put
Together, swallow in hot flames such splendor
Of ivory and iron and wood. Suddenly
The sounds changed, the Danes started
In new terror, cowering in their beds as the terrible
Screams of the Almighty's enemy sang
In the darkness, the horrible shrieks of pain
And defeat, the tears torn out of Grendel's
Taut throat, hell's captive caught in the arms
Of him who of all the men on earth
Was the strongest.

12

    That mighty protector of men
Meant to hold the monster till its life
Leaped out, knowing the fiend was no use
To anyone in Denmark. All of Beowulf's
795 Band had jumped from their beds, ancestral
Swords raised and ready, determined
To protect their prince if they could. Their courage
Was great but all wasted: they could hack at Grendel
From every side, trying to open
800 A path for his evil soul, but their points
Could not hurt him, the sharpest and hardest iron
Could not scratch at his skin, for that sin-stained demon
Had bewitched all men's weapons, laid spells
That blunted every mortal man's blade.
805 And yet his time had come, his days
Were over, his death near; down
To hell he would go, swept groaning and helpless
To the waiting hands of still worse fiends.
Now he discovered—once the afflictor
810 Of men, tormentor of their days—what it meant
To feud with Almighty God: Grendel
Saw that his strength was deserting him, his claws
Bound fast, Higlac's brave follower tearing at
His hands. The monster's hatred rose higher,

Beowulf

But his power had gone. He twisted in pain, 815
And the bleeding sinews deep in his shoulder
Snapped, muscle and bone split
And broke. The battle was over, Beowulf
Had been granted new glory: Grendel escaped,
But wounded as he was could flee to his den, 820
His miserable hole at the bottom of the marsh,
Only to die, to wait for the end
Of all his days. And after that bloody
Combat the Danes laughed with delight.
He who had come to them from across the sea, 825
Bold and strong-minded, had driven affliction
Off, purged Herot clean. He was happy,
Now, with that night's fierce work; the Danes
Had been served as he'd boasted he'd serve them;
    Beowulf,
A prince of the Geats, had killed Grendel, 830
Ended the grief, the sorrow, the suffering
Forced on Hrothgar's helpless people
By a bloodthirsty fiend. No Dane doubted
The victory, for the proof, hanging high
From the rafters where Beowulf had hung it, was
    the monster's 835
Arm, claw and shoulder and all.

13

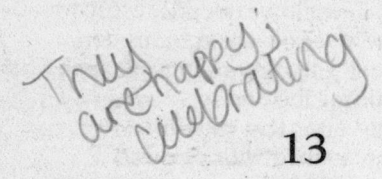

And then, in the morning, crowds surrounded
Herot, warriors coming to that hall
From faraway lands, princes and leaders
Of men hurrying to behold the monster's
Great staggering tracks. They gaped with no sense
Of sorrow, felt no regret for his suffering,
Went tracing his bloody footprints, his beaten
And lonely flight, to the edge of the lake
Where he'd dragged his corpselike way, doomed
And already weary of his vanishing life.
The water was bloody, steaming and boiling
In horrible pounding waves, heat
Sucked from his magic veins; but the swirling
Surf had covered his death, hidden
Deep in murky darkness his miserable
End, as hell opened to receive him.
   Then old and young rejoiced, turned back
From that happy pilgrimage, mounted their hard-
   hooved
Horses, high-spirited stallions, and rode them
Slowly toward Herot again, retelling
Beowulf's bravery as they jogged along.
And over and over they swore that nowhere
On earth or under the spreading sky
Or between the seas, neither south nor north,
Was there a warrior worthier to rule over men.

38

Beowulf

(But no one meant Beowulf's praise to belittle
Hrothgar, their kind and gracious king!)
    And sometimes, when the path ran straight and
        clear,
They would let their horses race, red 865
And brown and pale yellow backs streaming
Down the road. And sometimes a proud old soldier
Who had heard songs of the ancient heroes
And could sing them all through, story after story,
Would weave a net of words for Beowulf's 870
Victory, tying the knot of his verses
Smoothly, swiftly, into place with a poet's
Quick skill, singing his new song aloud
While he shaped it, and the old songs as well—
    Siegmund's
Adventures, familiar battles fought 875
By that glorious son of Vels. And struggles,
Too, against evil and treachery that no one
Had ever heard of, that no one knew
Except Fitla, who had fought at his uncle's side,
A brave young comrade carefully listening 880
When Siegmund's tongue unwound the wonders
He had worked, confiding in his closest friend.
There were tales of giants wiped from the earth
By Siegmund's might—and forever remembered,
Fame that would last him beyond life and death, 885
His daring battle with a treasure-rich dragon.
Heaving a hoary gray rock aside
Siegmund had gone down to the dragon alone,
Entered the hole where it hid and swung
His sword so savagely that it slit the creature 890
Through, pierced its flesh and pinned it
To a wall, hung it where his bright blade rested.
His courage and strength had earned him a kinglike
Treasure, brought gold and rich rings to his glorious
Hands. He loaded that precious hoard 895
On his ship and sailed off with a shining cargo.

Beowulf

And the dragon dissolved in its own fierce blood.
   No prince, no protector of his warriors, knew power
And fame and glory like Siegmund's; his name
And his treasures grew great. Hermod could have hoped
For at least as much; he was once the mightiest
Of men. But pride and defeat and betrayal
Sent him into exile with the Jutes, and he ended
His life on their swords. That life had been misery
After misery, and he spread sorrow as long
As he lived it, heaped troubles on his unhappy people's
Heads, ignored all wise men's warnings,
Ruled only with courage. A king
Born, entrusted with ancient treasures
And cities full of stronghearted soldiers,
His vanity swelled him so vile and rank
That he could hear no voices but his own. He deserved
To suffer and die. But Beowulf was a prince
Well-loved, followed in friendship, not fear;
Hermod's heart had been hollowed by sin.
   The horses ran, when they could, on the gravel
Path. Morning slid past and was gone.
The whole brave company came riding to Herot,
Anxious to celebrate Beowulf's success
And stare at that arm. And Hrothgar rose
From beside his wife and came with his courtiers
Crowded around him. And Welthow rose
And joined him, his wife and queen with her women,
All of them walking to that wonderful hall.

14

Hrothgar stood at the top of the stairway
And stared at Grendel's great claw, swinging
High from that gold-shining roof. Then he cried:
"Let God be thanked! Grendel's terrible
Anger hung over our heads too long,
Dropping down misery; but the Almighty makes miracles
When He pleases, wonder after wonder, and this world
Rests in His hands. I had given up hope,
Exhausted prayer, expected nothing
But misfortune forever. Herot was empty,
Bloody; the wisest and best of our people
Despaired as deeply, found hope no easier,
Knew nothing, no way to end this unequal
War of men and devils, warriors
And monstrous fiends. One man found it,
Came to Denmark and with the Lord's help
Did what none of the Danes could do,
Our wisdom, our strength, worthless without him.
The woman who bore him, whoever, wherever,
Alive now, or dead, knew the grace of the God
Of our fathers, was granted a son for her glory
And His. Beowulf, best of soldiers,
Let me take you to my heart, make you my son, too,
And love you: preserve this passionate peace

Between us. And take, in return, whatever
950 You may want from whatever I own. Warriors
Deserving far less have been granted as much,
Given gifts and honored, though they fought
No enemy like yours. Glory is now yours
Forever and ever; your courage has earned it,
And your strength. May God be as good to you
955   forever
As He has been to you here!"

                   Then Beowulf answered:
"What we did was what our hearts helped
Our hands to perform; we came to fight
960 With Grendel, our strength against his. I wish
I could show you, here in Herot, his corpse
Stretched on this floor! I twisted my fingers
Around his claw, ripped and tore at it
As hard as I could: I meant to kill him
965 Right here, hold him so tightly that his heart
Would stop, would break, his life spill
On this floor. But God's will was against me.
As hard as I held him he still pulled free
And ran, escaped from this hall with the strength
970 Fear had given him. But he offered me his arm
And his claw, saved his life yet left me
That prize. And paying even so willingly
For his freedom he still fled with nothing
But the end of his evil days, ran
975 With death pressing at his back, pain
Splitting his panicked heart, pulling him
Step by step into hell. Let him burn
In torment, lying and trembling, waiting
For the brightness of God to bring him his reward."
980 Unferth grew quiet, gave up quarreling over
Beowulf's old battles, stopped all his boasting
Once everyone saw proof of that prince's strength,
Grendel's huge claw swinging high
From Hrothgar's mead-hall roof, the fingers

Of that loathsome hand ending in nails 985
As hard as bright steel—so hard, they all said,
That not even the sharpest of swords could have cut
It through, broken it off the monster's
Arm and ended its life, as Beowulf
Had done armed with only his bare hands. 990

15

Then the king ordered Herot cleaned
And hung with decorations: hundreds of hands,
Men and women, hurried to make
The great hall ready. Golden tapestries
995 Were lined along the walls, for a host
Of visitors to see and take pleasure in. But that glorious
Building was bent and broken, its iron
Hinges cracked and sprung from their corners
All around the hall. Only
Its roof was undamaged when the bloodstained
1000 demon
Burst out of Herot, desperately breaking
Beowulf's grip, running wildly
From what no one escapes, struggle and writhe
As he will. Wanting to stay we go,
1005 All beings here on God's earth, wherever
It is written that we go, taking our bodies
From death's cold bed to the unbroken sleep
That follows life's feast.

      Then Hrothgar made his way
1010 To the hall; it was time, and his heart drew him
To the banquet. No victory was celebrated better,
By more or by better men and their king.

A mighty host, and famous, they lined
The benches, rejoicing; the king and Hrothulf,
His nephew, toasted each other, raised mead-cups   1015
High under Herot's great roof, their speech
Courteous and warm. King and people
Were one; none of the Danes was plotting,
Then, no treachery hid in their smiles.
   Healfdane's son gave Beowulf a golden   1020
Banner, a fitting flag to signal
His victory, and gave him, as well, a helmet,
And a coat of mail, and an ancient sword;
They were brought to him while the warriors
    watched. Beowulf
Drank to those presents, not ashamed to be praised, 1025
Richly rewarded in front of them all.
No ring-giver has given four such gifts,
Passed such treasures through his hands, with the
    grace
And warmth that Hrothgar showed. The helmet's
Brim was wound with bands of metal,   1030
Rounded ridges to protect whoever
Wore it from swords swung in the fiercest
Battles, shining iron edges
In hostile hands. And then the protector
Of warriors, lord of the Danes, ordered   1035
Eight horses led to the hall, and into it,
Eight steeds with golden bridles. One stood
With a jeweled saddle on its back, carved
Like the king's war-seat it was; it had carried
Hrothgar when that great son of Healfdane rode   1040
To war—and each time carried him wherever
The fighting was most fierce, and his followers had
    fallen.
Then Beowulf had been honored by both the gifts
Hrothgar could have given him, horses and weap-
    ons:
The king commanded him to use them well.   1045

Thus that guardian of Denmark's treasures
Had repaid a battle fought for his people
By giving noble gifts, had earned praise
For himself from those who try to know truth.

16

And more: the lord of Herot ordered
Treasure-gifts for each of the Geats
Who'd sailed with Beowulf and still sat beside him,
Ancient armor and swords—and for the one
Murdered by Grendel gold was carefully
Paid. The monster would have murdered again
And again had not God, and the hero's courage,
Turned fate aside. Then and now
Men must lie in their Maker's holy
Hands, moved only as He wills:
Our hearts must seek out that will. The world,
And its long days full of labor, brings good
And evil; all who remain here meet both.
  Hrothgar's hall resounded with the harp's
High call, with songs and laughter and the telling
Of tales, stories sung by the court
Poet as the joyful Danes drank
And listened, seated along their mead-benches.
He told them of Finn's people, attacking
Hnaf with no warning, half wiping out
That Danish tribe, and killing its king.
Finn's wife, Hnaf's sister, learned what good faith
Was worth to her husband: his honeyed words
And treachery cost her two belovèd lives,
Her son and her brother, both falling on spears
Guided by fate's hand. How she wept!

47

And when morning came she had reason to mourn,
To weep for her dead, her slaughtered son
And the bloody corpse of his uncle—both
The men she most dearly loved, and whose love
She could trust to protect her. But Finn's troops, too,
Had fallen to Danish spears: too few
Were left to drive the Danes to their death,
To force Hnaf's follower, Hengest, to flee
The hall where they'd fought and he'd stayed. Finn offered them,
Instead of more war, words of peace:
There would be no victory; they'd divide the hall
And the throne, half to the Danes, half
To Finn's followers. When gifts were given
Finn would give Hengest and his soldiers half,
Share shining rings, silver
And gold, with the Danes, both sides equal,
All of them richer, all of their purses
Heavy, every man's heart warm
With the comfort of gold.
                              Both sides accepted
Peace and agreed to keep it. Finn
Swore it with solemn oaths: what wise men
Had written was his word as well as theirs.
He and the brave Hengest would live
Like brothers; neither leader nor led would break
The truce, would not talk of evil things,
Remind the Danes that the man they served
Killed Hnaf, their lord. They had no king,
And no choice. And he swore that his sword would silence
Wagging tongues if Frisian warriors
Stirred up hatred, brought back the past.
    A funeral pyre was prepared, and gold
Was brought; Hnaf's dead body was dressed
For burning, and the others with him. Bloody
Mail shirts could be seen, and golden helmets,

Some carved with boar-heads, all battle-hard
And as useless, now, as the corpses that still wore
   them,
Soldier after soldier! Then Hnaf's sister,
Finn's sad wife, gave her son's body
To be burned in that fire; the flames charring   1115
His uncle would consume both kinsmen at once.
Then she wept again, and weeping sang
The dead's last praise. The Danish king
Was lifted into place, smoke went curling
Up, logs roared, open   1120
Wounds split and burst, skulls
Melted, blood came bubbling down,
And the greedy fire-demons drank flesh and bones
From the dead of both sides, until nothing was left.

17

Finn released a few of his soldiers,
Allowed them to return to their distant towns
And estates. Hengest lived the whole stormy
Winter through, there with Finn,
Whom he hated. But his heart lived in Denmark—
Which he and the other survivors could not visit,
Could not sail to, as long as the wind-whipped sea
Crashed and whirled, or while winter's cold hands
Froze the water hard, tied it
In icy knots. They would wait for the new year,
For spring to come following the sun, melting
The old year away and reopening the ocean.
Winter was over, the earth grew lovely,
And Hengest dreamed of his home—but revenge
Came first, settling his bitter feud
With Finn, whose bloody sword he could never
Forget. He planned, he waited, wove plans
And waited. Then a Danish warrior dropped
A sword in his lap, a weapon Finn
And his men remembered and feared, and the time
Had come, and Hengest rose, hearing
The Danes' murmur, and drove his new sword
Into Finn's belly, butchering that king
Under his own roof. And the Danes rose,
Their hearts full of Finn's treachery,

Beowulf

And the misery he'd brought them, their sword arms restless
And eager. The hall they'd shared with their enemies
Ran red with enemy blood and bodies
Rolled on the floor beside Finn. They took
The queen, looted everything they could find
That belonged to her dead husband, loaded
Their ship with rings, necklaces, shining
Jewels wonderfully worked, and sailed
Bringing treasure and a willing captive to the land
She'd left and had longed for, alone no longer.

The singer finished his song; his listeners
Laughed and drank, their pleasure loud
In that hall. The cup-bearers hurried with their sparkling
Vessels. And then the queen, Welthow, wearing her bright crown,
Appeared among them, came to Hrothgar and Hrothulf, his nephew,
Seated peacefully together, their friendship and Hrothulf's good faith still unbroken.
And Unferth sat at Hrothgar's feet; everyone trusted him,
Believed in his courage, although he'd spilled his relatives' blood.
Then Welthow spoke:
                "Accept this cup,
My lord and king! May happiness come
To the Danes' great ring-giver; may the Geats receive
Mild words from your mouth, words they have earned!
Let gifts flow freely from your open hands,
Treasures your armies have brought you from all over
The world. I have heard that the greatest of the Geats

Now rests in your heart like a son. Herot
Stands purged, restored by his strength: celebrate
His courage, rejoice and be generous while a kingdom
Sits in your palm, a people and power
1180 That death will steal. But your sons will be safe,
Sheltered in Hrothulf's gracious protection,
If fate takes their father while Hrothulf is alive;
I know your nephew's kindness, I know
He'll repay in kind the goodness you have shown him,
1185 Support your two young sons as you
And I sustained him in his own early days,
His father dead and he but a boy."

    Then she walked to the bench where Hrethric and Hrothmund,
Her two sons, sat together; Beowulf,
1190 Prince of the Geats, was seated between them;
Crossing the hall she sat quietly at their side.

18

They brought a foaming cup and offered it
To Beowulf; it was taken and given in friendship.
And he was given a mail shirt, and golden arm-
    bands,
And the most beautiful necklace known to men: *1195*
Nowhere in any treasure-hoard anywhere
On earth was there anything like it, not since
Hama carried the Brosings' necklace
Home to his glorious city, saved
Its tight-carved jewels, and his skin, and his soul   *1200*
From Ermric's treachery, and then came to God.
Higlac had it next, Swerting's
Grandson; defending the golden hoard
His battle-hard hands had won for him, the Geats'
Proud king lost it, was carried away   *1205*
By fate when too much pride made him feud
With the Frisians. He had asked for misery; it was
    granted him.
He'd borne those precious stones on a ship's
Broad back; he fell beneath his shield.
His body, and his shining coat of mail,   *1210*
And that necklace, all lay for Franks to pluck,
For jackal warriors to find when they walked
    through
The rows of corpses; Geats, and their king,
Lay slaughtered wherever the robbers looked.

53

54   *Beowulf*

1215   The warriors shouted. And Welthow spoke:
         "Wear these bright jewels, belovèd Beowulf;
       Enjoy them, and the rings, and the gold, O fortu-
           nate young
       Warrior; grow richer, let your fame and your
           strength
       Go hand in hand; and lend these two boys
1220   Your wise and gentle heart! I'll remember your
       Kindness. Your glory is too great to forget:
       It will last forever, wherever the earth
       Is surrounded by the sea, the winds' home,
       And waves lap at its walls. Be happy
1225   For as long as you live! Your good fortune warms
       My soul. Spread your blessèd protection
       Across my son, and my king's son!
       All men speak softly, here, speak mildly
       And trust their neighbors, protect their lord,
1230   Are loyal followers who would fight as joyfully
       As they drink. May your heart help you do as I
           ask!"
         She returned to her seat. The soldiers ate
       And drank like kings. The savage fate
       Decreed for them hung dark and unknown, what
           would follow
       After nightfall, when Hrothgar withdrew from the
1235   hall,
       Sought his bed and left his soldiers
       To theirs. Herot would house a host
       Of men, that night, as it had been meant to do.
       They stacked away the benches, spread out
       Blankets and pillows. But those beer-drinking sleep-
1240   ers
       Lay down with death beside their beds.
       They slept with their shining shields at the edge
       Of their pillows; the hall was filled with helmets
       Hanging near motionless heads; spears
1245   Stood by their hands, their hammered mail shirts
       Covered their chests. It was the Danes' custom

To be ready for war, wherever they rested,
At home or in foreign lands, at their lord's
Quick call if he needed them, if trouble came
To their king. They knew how soldiers must live!

19

They sank into sleep. The price of that evening's
Rest was too high for the Dane who bought it
With his life, paying as others had paid
When Grendel inhabited Herot, the hall
1255 His till his crimes pulled him into hell.
And now it was known that a monster had died
But a monster still lived, and meant revenge.
She'd brooded on her loss, misery had brewed
In her heart, that female horror, Grendel's
1260 Mother, living in the murky cold lake
Assigned her since Cain had killed his only
Brother, slain his father's son
With an angry sword. God drove him off,
Outlawed him to the dry and barren desert,
And branded him with a murderer's mark. And
1265   he bore
A race of fiends accursed like their father;
So Grendel was drawn to Herot, an outcast
Come to meet the man who awaited him.
He'd snatched at Beowulf's arm, but that prince
Remembered God's grace and the strength He'd
1270   given him
And relied on the Lord for all the help,
The comfort and support he would need. He killed
The monster, as God had meant him to do,
Tore the fiend apart and forced him

To run as rapidly as he could toward death's   1275
Cold waiting hands. His mother's sad heart,
And her greed, drove her from her den on the dangerous
Pathway of revenge.
                    So she reached Herot,
Where the Danes slept as though already dead;   1280
Her visit ended their good fortune, reversed
The bright vane of their luck. No female, no matter
How fierce, could have come with a man's strength,
Fought with the power and courage men fight with,
Smashing their shining swords, their bloody,   1285
Hammer-forged blades onto boar-headed helmets,
Slashing and stabbing with the sharpest of points.
The soldiers raised their shields and drew
Those gleaming swords, swung them above
The piled-up benches, leaving their mail shirts   1290
And their helmets where they'd lain when the terror took hold of them.
To save her life she moved still faster,
Took a single victim and fled from the hall,
Running to the moors, discovered, but her supper
Assured, sheltered in her dripping claws.   1295
She'd taken Hrothgar's closest friend,
The man he most loved of all men on earth;
She'd killed a glorious soldier, cut
A noble life short. No Geat could have stopped her:
Beowulf and his band had been given better   1300
Beds; sleep had come to them in a different
Hall. Then all Herot burst into shouts:
She had carried off Grendel's claw. Sorrow
Had returned to Denmark. They'd traded deaths,
Danes and monsters, and no one had won,   1305
Both had lost!
              The wise old king
Trembled in anger and grief, his dearest
Friend and adviser dead. Beowulf

58   *Beowulf*

¹³¹⁰ Was sent for at once: a messenger went swiftly
To his rooms and brought him. He came, his band
About him, as dawn was breaking through,
The best of all warriors, walking to where Hrothgar
Sat waiting, the gray-haired king wondering
¹³¹⁵ If God would ever end this misery. kenning
The Geats tramped quickly through the hall; their steps
Beat and echoed in the silence. Beowulf
Rehearsed the words he would want with Hrothgar;
He'd ask the Danes' great lord if all
¹³²⁰ Were at peace, if the night had passed quietly.

20

Hrothgar answered him, protector of his people:
"There's no happiness to ask about! Anguish
    has descended
On the Danes. Esher is dead, Ermlaf's
Older brother and my own most trusted
Counselor and friend, my comrade, when we went   *1325*
Into battle, who'd beaten back enemy swords,
Standing at my side. All my soldiers
Should be as he was, their hearts as brave
And as wise! Another wandering fiend
Has found him in Herot, murdered him, fled   *1330*
With his corpse: he'll be eaten, his flesh become
A horrible feast—and who knows where
The beast may be hiding, its belly stuffed full?
She's taking revenge for your victory over Grendel,
For your strength, your mighty grip, and that mon-
    ster's   *1335*
Death. For years he'd been preying on my people;
You came, he was dead in a single day,
And now there's another one, a second hungry
Fiend, determined to avenge the first,
A monster willing and more than able   *1340*
To bring us more sorrow—or so it must seem
To the many men mourning that noble
Treasure-giver, for all men were treated

59

Nobly by those hands now forever closed.

1345 "I've heard that my people, peasants working
In the fields, have seen a pair of such fiends
Wandering in the moors and marshes, giant
Monsters living in those desert lands.
And they've said to my wise men that, as well as
    they could see,
1350 One of the devils was a female creature.
The other, they say, walked through the wilderness
Like a man—but mightier than any man.
They were frightened, and they fled, hoping to
    find help
In Herot. They named the huge one Grendel:
1355 If he had a father no one knew him,
Or whether there'd been others before these two,
Hidden evil before hidden evil.
They live in secret places, windy
Cliffs, wolf-dens where water pours
1360 From the rocks, then runs underground, where mist
Steams like black clouds, and the groves of trees
Growing out over their lake are all covered
With frozen spray, and wind down snakelike
Roots that reach as far as the water
1365 And help keep it dark. At night that lake
Burns like a torch. No one knows its bottom,
No wisdom reaches such depths. A deer,
Hunted through the woods by packs of hounds,
A stag with great horns, though driven through
    the forest
1370 From faraway places, prefers to die
On those shores, refuses to save its life
In that water. It isn't far, nor is it
A pleasant spot! When the wind stirs
And storms, waves splash toward the sky,
1375 As dark as the air, as black as the rain
That the heavens weep. Our only help,
Again, lies with you. Grendel's mother
Is hidden in her terrible home, in a place

You've not seen. Seek it, if you dare! Save us,
Once more, and again twisted gold, 1380
Heaped-up ancient treasure, will reward you
For the battle you win!"

21

Beowulf spoke:
"Let your sorrow end! It is better for us all
To avenge our friends, not mourn them forever.
Each of us will come to the end of this life
On earth; he who can earn it should fight
For the glory of his name; fame after death
Is the noblest of goals. Arise, guardian
Of this kingdom, let us go, as quickly as we can,
And have a look at this lady monster.
I promise you this: she'll find no shelter,
No hole in the ground, no towering tree,
No deep bottom of a lake, where her sins can hide.
Be patient for one more day of misery;
I ask for no longer."
                    The old king leaped
To his feet, gave thanks to God for such words.
Then Hrothgar's horse was brought, saddled
And bridled. The Danes' wise ruler rode,
Stately and splendid; shield-bearing soldiers
Marched at his side. The monster's tracks
Led them through the forest; they followed her heavy
Feet, that had swept straight across
The shadowy wasteland, her burden the lifeless
Body of the best of Hrothgar's men.
The trail took them up towering, rocky

Hills, and over narrow, winding
Paths they had never seen, down steep
And slippery cliffs where creatures from deep
In the earth hid in their holes. Hrothgar
Rode in front, with a few of his most knowing
Men, to find their way. Then suddenly,
Where clumps of trees bent across
Cold gray stones, they came to a dismal
Wood; below them was the lake, its water
Bloody and bubbling. And the Danes shivered,
Miserable, mighty men tormented
By grief, seeing, there on that cliff
Above the water, Esher's bloody
Head. They looked down at the lake, felt
How its heat rose up, watched the waves'
Bloodstained swirling. Their battle horns sounded,
Then sounded again. Then they set down their weapons.

They could see the water crawling with snakes,
Fantastic serpents swimming in the boiling
Lake, and sea beasts lying on the rocks
—The kind that infest the ocean, in the early
Dawn, often ending some ship's
Journey with their wild jaws. They rushed
Angrily out of sight, when the battle horns blew.
Beowulf aimed an arrow at one
Of the beasts, swimming sluggishly away,
And the point pierced its hide, stabbed
To its heart; its life leaked out, death
Swept it off. Quickly, before
The dying monster could escape, they hooked
Its thrashing body with their curved boar-spears,
Fought it to land, drew it up on the bluff,
Then stood and stared at the incredible wave-roamer,
Covered with strange scales and horrible. Then Beowulf
Began to fasten on his armor,

Not afraid for his life but knowing the woven
Mail, with its hammered links, could save
1445 That life when he lowered himself into the lake,
Keep slimy monsters' claws from snatching at
His heart, preserve him for the battle he was sent
To fight. Hrothgar's helmet would defend him;
That ancient, shining treasure, encircled
1450 With hard-rolled metal, set there by some smith's
Long-dead hand, would block all battle
Swords, stop all blades from cutting at him
When he'd swum toward the bottom, gone down in the surging
Water, deep toward the swirling sands.
1455 And Unferth helped him, Hrothgar's courtier
Lent him a famous weapon, a fine,
Hilted old sword named Hrunting; it had
An iron blade, etched and shining
And hardened in blood. No one who'd worn it
1460 Into battle, swung it in dangerous places,
Daring and brave, had ever been deserted—
Nor was Beowulf's journey the first time it was taken
To an enemy's camp, or asked to support
Some hero's courage and win him glory.
1465 Unferth had tried to forget his greeting
To Beowulf, his drunken speech of welcome;
A mighty warrior, he lent his weapon
To a better one. Only Beowulf would risk
His life in that lake; Unferth was afraid,
1470 Gave up that chance to work wonders, win glory
And a hero's fame. But Beowulf and fear
Were strangers; he stood ready to dive into battle.

22

Then Edgetho's brave son spoke:
                                    "Remember,
Hrothgar, O knowing king, now
When my danger is near, the warm words we uttered,
And if your enemy should end my life
Then be, O generous prince, forever
The father and protector of all whom I leave
Behind me, here in your hands, my belovèd
Comrades left with no leader, their leader
Dead. And the precious gifts you gave me,
My friend, send them to Higlac. May he see
In their golden brightness, the Geats' great lord
Gazing at your treasure, that here in Denmark
I found a noble protector, a giver
Of rings whose rewards I won and briefly
Relished. And you, Unferth, let
My famous old sword stay in your hands:
I shall shape glory with Hrunting, or death
Will hurry me from this earth!"
                                    As his words ended
He leaped into the lake, would not wait for anyone's
Answer; the heaving water covered him
Over. For hours he sank through the waves;
At last he saw the mud of the bottom.

And all at once the greedy she-wolf
Who'd ruled those waters for half a hundred
Years discovered him, saw that a creature
From above had come to explore the bottom
Of her wet world. She welcomed him in her claws,
Clutched at him savagely but could not harm him,
Tried to work her fingers through the tight
Ring-woven mail on his breast, but tore
And scratched in vain. Then she carried him, armor
And sword and all, to her home; he struggled
To free his weapon, and failed. The fight
Brought other monsters swimming to see
Her catch, a host of sea beasts who beat at
His mail shirt, stabbing with tusks and teeth
As they followed along. Then he realized, suddenly,
That she'd brought him into someone's battle-hall,
And there the water's heat could not hurt him,
Nor anything in the lake attack him through
The building's high-arching roof. A brilliant
Light burned all around him, the lake
Itself like a fiery flame.
                 Then he saw
The mighty water witch, and swung his sword,
His ring-marked blade, straight at her head;
The iron sang its fierce song,
Sang Beowulf's strength. But her guest
Discovered that no sword could slice her evil
Skin, that Hrunting could not hurt her, was useless
Now when he needed it. They wrestled, she ripped
And tore and clawed at him, bit holes in his helmet,
And that, too, failed him; for the first time in years
Of being worn to war it would earn no glory;
It was the last time anyone would wear it. But Beowulf
Longed only for fame, leaped back
Into battle. He tossed his sword aside,
Angry; the steel-edged blade lay where
He'd dropped it. If weapons were useless he'd use

His hands, the strength in his fingers. So fame
Comes to the men who mean to win it   *1535*
And care about nothing else! He raised
His arms and seized her by the shoulder; anger
Doubled his strength, he threw her to the floor.
She fell, Grendel's fierce mother, and the Geats'
Proud prince was ready to leap on her. But she rose   *1540*
At once and repaid him with her clutching claws,
Wildly tearing at him. He was weary, that best
And strongest of soldiers; his feet stumbled
And in an instant she had him down, held helpless.
Squatting with her weight on his stomach, she drew   *1545*
A dagger, brown with dried blood, and prepared
To avenge her only son. But he was stretched
On his back, and her stabbing blade was blunted
By the woven mail shirt he wore on his chest.
The hammered links held; the point   *1550*
Could not touch him. He'd have traveled to the
    bottom of the earth,
Edgetho's son, and died there, if that shining
Woven metal had not helped—and Holy
God, who sent him victory, gave judgment
For truth and right, Ruler of the Heavens,   *1555*
Once Beowulf was back on his feet and fighting.

23

Then he saw, hanging on the wall, a heavy
Sword, hammered by giants, strong
And blessed with their magic, the best of all weapons
1560 But so massive that no ordinary man could lift
Its carved and decorated length. He drew it
From its scabbard, broke the chain on its hilt,
And then, savage, now, angry
And desperate, lifted it high over his head
1565 And struck with all the strength he had left,
Caught her in the neck and cut it through,
Broke bones and all. Her body fell
To the floor, lifeless, the sword was wet
With her blood, and Beowulf rejoiced at the sight.
1570 The brilliant light shone, suddenly,
As though burning in that hall, and as bright as Heaven's
Own candle, lit in the sky. He looked
At her home, then following along the wall
Went walking, his hands tight on the sword,
1575 His heart still angry. He was hunting another
Dead monster, and took his weapon with him
For final revenge against Grendel's vicious
Attacks, his nighttime raids, over
And over, coming to Herot when Hrothgar's
1580 Men slept, killing them in their beds,

Beowulf

Eating some on the spot, fifteen
Or more, and running to his loathsome moor
With another such sickening meal waiting
In his pouch. But Beowulf repaid him for those visits,
Found him lying dead in his corner,   1585
Armless, exactly as that fierce fighter
Had sent him out from Herot, then struck off
His head with a single swift blow. The body
Jerked for the last time, then lay still.
    The wise old warriors who surrounded Hrothgar, 1590
Like him staring into the monsters' lake,
Saw the waves surging and blood
Spurting through. They spoke about Beowulf,
All the graybeards, whispered together
And said that hope was gone, that the hero   1595
Had lost fame and his life at once, and would never
Return to the living, come back as triumphant
As he had left; almost all agreed that Grendel's
Mighty mother, the she-wolf, had killed him.
The sun slid over past noon, went further   1600
Down. The Danes gave up, left
The lake and went home, Hrothgar with them.
The Geats stayed, sat sadly, watching,
Imagining they saw their lord but not believing
They would ever see him again.
                            —Then the sword 1605
Melted, blood-soaked, dripping down
Like water, disappearing like ice when the world's
Eternal Lord loosens invisible
Fetters and unwinds icicles and frost
As only He can, He who rules   1610
Time and seasons, He who is truly
God. The monsters' hall was full of
Rich treasures, but all that Beowulf took
Was Grendel's head and the hilt of the giants'
Jeweled sword; the rest of that ring-marked   1615
Blade had dissolved in Grendel's steaming

Blood, boiling even after his death.
And then the battle's only survivor
Swam up and away from those silent corpses;
1620 The water was calm and clean, the whole
Huge lake peaceful once the demons who'd lived in it
Were dead.
        Then that noble protector of all seamen
Swam to land, rejoicing in the heavy
1625 Burdens he was bringing with him. He
And all his glorious band of Geats
Thanked God that their leader had come back unharmed;
They left the lake together. The Geats
Carried Beowulf's helmet, and his mail shirt.
1630 Behind them the water slowly thickened
As the monsters' blood came seeping up.
They walked quickly, happily, across
Roads all of them remembered, left
The lake and the cliffs alongside it, brave men
1635 Staggering under the weight of Grendel's skull,
Too heavy for fewer than four of them to handle—
Two on each side of the spear jammed through it—
Yet proud of their ugly load and determined
That the Danes, seated in Herot, should see it.
1640 Soon, fourteen Geats arrived
At the hall, bold and warlike, and with Beowulf,
Their lord and leader, they walked on the mead-hall
Green. Then the Geats' brave prince entered
Herot, covered with glory for the daring
1645 Battles he had fought; he sought Hrothgar
To salute him and show Grendel's head.
He carried that terrible trophy by the hair,
Brought it straight to where the Danes sat,
Drinking, the queen among them. It was a weird
1650 And wonderful sight, and the warriors stared.

After Beowulf kills Grendel's mother He tells the tale

24

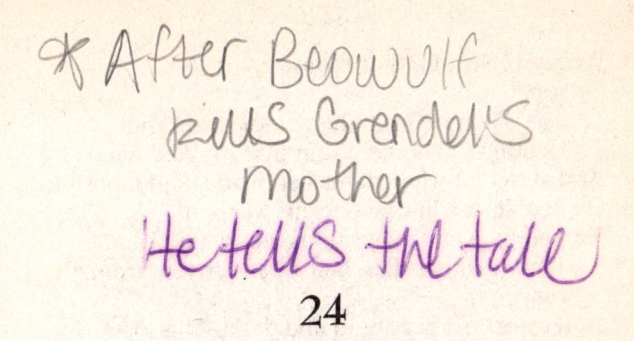

Beowulf spoke:
                "Hrothgar! Behold,
Great Healfdane's son, this glorious sign
Of victory, brought you by joyful Geats.
My life was almost lost, fighting for it,   1655
Struggling under water: I'd have been dead at once,
And the fight finished, the she-devil victorious,
If our Father in Heaven had not helped me. Hrunt-
   ing, *Appositive*
Unferth's noble weapon, could do nothing,
Nor could I, until the Ruler of the world   1660
Showed me, hanging shining and beautiful
On a wall, a mighty old sword—so God   *God helped him*
Gives guidance to those who can find it from no one
Else. I used the weapon He had offered me,
Drew it and, when I could, swung it, killed   1665
The monstrous hag in her own home.
Then the ring-marked blade burned away,
As that boiling blood spilled out. I carried
Off all that was left, this hilt.
I've avenged their crimes, and the Danes they've
   killed.   1670
And I promise you that whoever sleeps in Herot
—You, your brave soldiers, anyone
Of all the people in Denmark, old
Or young—they, and you, may now sleep

1675 Without fear of either monster, mother
Or son."
　　　　　Then he gave the golden sword hilt
To Hrothgar, who held it in his wrinkled hands
And stared at what giants had made, and monsters
1680 Owned; it was his, an ancient weapon
Shaped by wonderful smiths, now that Grendel
And his evil mother had been driven from the earth,
God's enemies scattered and dead. That best
Of swords belonged to the best of Denmark's
1685 Rulers, the wisest ring-giver Danish
Warriors had ever known. The old king
Bent close to the handle of the ancient relic,
And saw written there the story of ancient wars
Between good and evil, the opening of the waters,
1690 The Flood sweeping giants away, how they suffered
And died, that race who hated the Ruler
Of us all and received judgment from His hands,
Surging waves that found them wherever
They fled. And Hrothgar saw runic letters
1695 Clearly carved in that shining hilt,
Spelling its original owner's name,
He for whom it was made, with its twisted
Handle and snakelike carvings. Then he spoke,
Healfdane's son, and everyone was silent.
1700 "What I say, speaking from a full memory
And after a life spent in seeking
What was right for my people, is this: this prince
Of the Geats, Beowulf, was born a better
Man! Your fame is everywhere, my friend,
Reaches to the ends of the earth, and you hold it
1705 　　in your heart wisely,
Patient with your strength and our weakness. What
　　I said I will do, I will do,
In the name of the friendship we've sworn. Your
　　strength must solace your people,
Now, and mine no longer.

Bad King

"Be not
As Hermod once was to my people, too proud   1710
To care what their hearts hid, bringing them
Only destruction and slaughter. In his mad
Rages he killed them himself, comrades
And followers who ate at his table. At the end
He was alone, knew none of the joys of life   1715
With other men, a famous ruler
Granted greater strength than anyone
Alive in his day but dark and bloodthirsty
In spirit. He shared out no treasure, showed
His soldiers no road to riches and fame.   1720
And then that affliction on his people's face
Suffered horribly for his sins. Be taught
By his lesson, learn what a king must be:
I tell his tale, old as I am,
Only for you.   1725
             "Our eternal Lord
Grants some men wisdom, some wealth, makes others
Great. The world is God's, He allows
A man to grow famous, and his family rich,
Gives him land and towns to rule   1730
And delight in, lets his kingdom reach
As far as the world runs—and who
In human unwisdom, in the middle of such power,
Remembers that it all will end, and too soon?
Prosperity, prosperity, prosperity: nothing   1735
Troubles him, no sickness, not passing time,
No sorrows, no sudden war breaking
Out of nowhere, but all the world turns
When he spins it. How can he know when he sins?

25

1740 "And then pride grows in his heart, planted
Quietly but flourishing. And while the keeper of his soul
Sleeps on, while conscience rests and the world
Turns faster a murderer creeps closer, comes carrying
A tight-strung bow with terrible arrows.
1745 And those sharp points strike home, are shot
In his breast, under his helmet. He's helpless.
And so the Devil's dark urgings wound him, for he can't
Remember how he clung to the rotting wealth
Of this world, how he clawed to keep it, how he earned
1750 No honor, no glory, in giving golden
Rings, how he forgot the future glory
God gave him at his birth, and forgetting did not care.
And finally his body fails him, these bones
And flesh quickened by God fall
1755 And die—and some other soul inherits
His place in Heaven, some open-handed
Giver of old treasures, who takes no delight
In mere gold. Guard against such wickedness,
Belovèd Beowulf, best of warriors, APPOSITIVE
1760 And choose, instead, eternal happiness;

Beowulf

Push away pride! Your strength, your power,
Are yours for how many years? Soon
You'll return them where they came from, sickness
    or a sword's edge
Will end them, or a grasping fire, or the flight
Of a spear, or surging waves, or a knife's   1765
Bite, or the terror of old age, or your eyes
Darkening over. It will come, death
Comes faster than you think, no one can flee it.

   "So I have led the Danes for half
A hundred years, protected them from all peoples   1770
On this earth, my sword and my spear so ready
That no one anywhere under God's high sun
Was eager to wage war here in Denmark.
And here, here, too, the change has come,
And we wept for our dead when Grendel invaded   1775
Herot, my enemy raided this hall;
My sorrow, my grief, was as great and lasting
As it was helpless. Then thanks be given to God,
Eternal Lord of us all: you came
And that endless misery was over and I lived,   1780
Now, to behold this bloody head!
Go in, go in: feast, be as happy
As your fame deserves. When morning shines
We shall each have owned more of my treasures."

   Beowulf obeyed him, entered Herot   1785
Cheerfully and took his place at the table.
And once again Danes and Geats
Feasted together, a host of famous
Warriors in a single hall.—Then the web
Of darkness fell and it was night. They rose;   1790
Hrothgar, the gray-haired old Dane, was heavy
With sleep. And Beowulf was glad that a bed
Was waiting, the bravest of warriors exhausted
With the work he'd done. A Danish servant
Showed him the road to that far-off, quiet   1795
Country where sleep would come and take him
And his followers; Hrothgar's visitors were well

Cared for, whatever they needed was theirs.
　　　　Then Beowulf rested; Herot rose high
1800 Above him, gleaming in the darkness; the Geats
　　　Slept till a black-feathered raven sang
　　　His cheerful song and the shining sun
　　　Burned away shadows. And those seafarers hurried
　　　From their beds, anxious to begin the voyage
1805 Home, ready to start, their hearts
　　　Already sailing on a ship's swift back.
　　　　Then Unferth came, with Hrunting, his famous
　　　Sword, and offered it to Beowulf, asked him
　　　To accept a precious gift. The prince
1810 Took it, thanked him, and declared the weapon
　　　One he was proud to own; his words
　　　Blamed it for nothing, were spoken like the hero
　　　He was! The war-gear was ready, the Geats
　　　Were armored and eager to be gone. Quickly,
1815 Beowulf sought Hrothgar's throne, where the king
　　　Sat waiting for his famous visitor's farewell.

26

Beowulf spoke:
                  "We crossed the sea
To come here; it is time to return, to go back
To our belovèd lord, Higlac. Denmark   1820
Was a gracious host; you welcomed us warmly.
Anything I can do, here on this earth,
To earn your love, O great king, anything
More than I have done, battles I can fight
In your honor, summon me, I will come as I came 1825
Once before. If I hear, from across the ocean,
That your neighbors have threatened you with war,
    or oppressed you
As enemies once oppressed you, here, I will bring
A thousand warriors, a thousand armed Geats
To protect your throne. I trust Higlac: 1830
Our king is young, but if I need his help
To better help you, to lend you our strength,
Our battle-sharp spears, to shield you and honor
    you
As you deserve, I know his words and his deeds
Will support me. And someday, if your oldest son, 1835
Hrethric, comes visiting our court, he will find
A host of good friends among the Geats:
No one who goes visiting far-off lands
Is more welcome than a strong and noble warrior."

1840 Hrothgar replied:
               "All-knowing God
Must have sent you such words; nothing so wise
From a warrior so young has ever reached
These ancient ears. Your hands are strong,
1845 Your heart and your lips are knowing! If your lord,
Hrethel's son, is slain by a spear,
Or falls sick and dies, or is killed by a sword,
And you have survived whatever battle
Sweeps him off, I say that the Geats
1850 Could do no better, find no man better
Suited to be king, keeper of warriors
And their treasure, than you—if you take the throne
They will surely offer you. Belovèd Beowulf,
You please me more the longer I can keep you
1855 Here in Denmark. You've turned Danes
And Geats into brothers, brought peace where once
There was war, and sealed friendship with affection.
This will last as long as I live, and am king here:
We will share our treasures, greeting travelers
1860 From across the sea with outstretched hands;
Ring-prowed ships will carry our gifts
And the tokens of our love. Your people live
By the old ways, their hearts, like ours, are forever
Open to their friends, but firmly closed
1865 Against their enemies."
                    Then he gave the Geats'
Prince a dozen new gifts, prayed
For his safety, commanded him to seek his people,
Yet not to delay too long in visiting
1870 Hrothgar once more. The old king kissed him,
Held that best of all warriors by the shoulder
And wept, unable to hold back his tears.
Gray and wise, he knew how slim
Were his chances of ever greeting Beowulf
1875 Again, but seeing his face he was forced
To hope. His love was too warm to be hidden,
His tears came running too quickly to be checked;

His very blood burned with longing.
And then Beowulf left him, left Herot, walked
Across the green in his golden armor, 1880
Exulting in the treasures heaped high in his arms.
His ship was at anchor; he had it ready to sail.
And so Hrothgar's rich treasures would leave him,
   travel
Far from that perfect king, without fault
Or blame until winter had followed winter 1885
And age had stolen his strength, spirited it
Off, as it steals from many men.

27

Then the band of Geats, young and brave,
Marching in their ring-locked armor, reached
1890 The shore. The coast-guard saw them coming
And about to go, as he'd seen them before;
He hurried down the hillside, whipping
His horse, but this time shouted no challenge,
Told them only how the Geats would be watching,
1895 Too, and would welcome such warriors in shining
Mail. Their broad-beamed ship lay bobbing
At the edge of the sand: they loaded it high
With armor and horses and all the rich treasure
It could hold. The mast stood high and straight
1900 Over heaped-up wealth—Hrothgar's, and now theirs.
Beowulf rewarded the boat's watchman,
Who had stayed behind, with a sword that had hammered
Gold wound on its handle: the weapon
Brought him honor. Then the ship left shore, left Denmark,
1905 Traveled through deep water. Deck timbers creaked,
And the wind billowing through the sail stretched
From the mast, tied tight with ropes, did not hold them
Back, did not keep the ring-prowed ship
From foaming swiftly through the waves, the sea
1910 Currents, across the wide ocean until

Beowulf

They could see familiar headlands, cliffs
That sprang out of Geatish soil. Driven
By the wind the ship rammed high on the shore.
Harbor guards came running to greet them,
Men who for days had waited and watched   1915
For their belovèd comrades to come crossing the waves;
They anchored the high-bowed ship, moored it
Close to the shore, where the booming sea
Could not pull it loose and lead it away.
Then they carried up the golden armor,   1920
The ancient swords, the jewels, brought them
To Higlac's home, their ring-giver's hall
Near the sea, where he lived surrounded
By his followers.
    He was a famous king, with a fitting   1925
High hall and a wife, Higd, young
But wise and knowing beyond her years.
She was Hareth's daughter, a noble queen
With none of the niggardly ways of women
Like Thrith. Higd gave the Geats gifts   1930
With open hands. But Thrith was too proud,
An imperious princess with a vicious tongue
And so fierce and wild that her father's followers
Averted their eyes as she passed, knowing
That if anyone but their king watched where she walked   1935
Her hands would shape a noose to fit
Their necks. She would lie, her father's lieutenants
Would write out her warrants, and he who had stared
Would end his life on the edge of an ancient
Sword. And how great a sin for a woman,   1940
Whether fair or black, to create fear
And destruction, for a woman, who should walk in the ways
Of peace, to kill with pretended insults.
But Hemming's kinsman tamed her: his hall-guests

¹⁹⁴⁵ Told a different story, spread the news
That Thrith had forgotten her gory tricks
Once her wise father had sent her to a wedding
With Offa, married her to that brave young soldier,
Sent her across the yellow-green sea
¹⁹⁵⁰ To that gold-adorned champion, a fierce fighter
In war or peace. They praised her, now,
For her generous heart, and her goodness, and the high
And most noble paths she walked, filled
With adoring love for that leader of warriors,
¹⁹⁵⁵ Her husband; he was a man as brave and strong
And good, it is said, as anyone on this earth,
A spear-bold soldier who knew no fear,
Exalted with gifts, victorious in war,
A king who ruled his native land
¹⁹⁶⁰ Wisely and well. Emer was his son,
Hemming's kinsman, Garmund's grandson,
A powerful swordsman and his warriors' shield.

28

Then Beowulf and his men went walking along
The shore, down the broad strip of sand.
The world's bright candle shone, hurrying
Up from the south. It was a short journey
From their ship to Higlac's home, to the hall
Where their king, Ongentho's killer, lived
With his warriors and gave treasures away. They walked
Quickly. The young king knew
They were back, Beowulf and his handful of brave
Men, come safely home; he sat,
Now, waiting to see them, to greet
His battle-comrades when they arrived at his court.
   They came. And when Beowulf had bowed to his lord,
And standing in front of the throne had solemnly
Spoken loyal words, Higlac
Ordered him to sit at his side—he
Who had survived, sailed home victorious, next to
His kinsman and king. Mead cups were filled
And Hareth's daughter took them through the hall,
Carried ale to her husband's comrades.
Higlac, unable to stay silent, anxious
To know how Beowulf's adventure had gone,
Began to question him, courteous but eager

[handwritten: Beowulf retells his battles]

To be told everything.
                    "Belovèd Beowulf,
Tell us what your trip to far-off places
Brought you, your sudden expedition on the salty
1990 Waves, your search for war in Herot?
Did you end Hrothgar's hopeless misery,
Could you help that glorious king? Grendel's
Savagery lay heavy on my heart but I was afraid
To let you go to him; for a long time
1995 I held you here, kept you safe,
Forced you to make the Danes fight
Their own battles. God be praised
That my eyes have beheld you once more, unharmed!"
Beowulf spoke, Edgetho's brave son: *[handwritten: Appositive]*
2000 "My lord Higlac, my meeting with Grendel
And the nighttime battle we fought are known
To everyone in Denmark, where the monster was once
The uncrowned ruler, murdering and eating
Hrothgar's people, forever bringing them
2005 Misery. I ended his reign, avenged
His crimes so completely in the crashing darkness
That not even the oldest of his evil kind
Will ever boast, lying in sin
And deceit, that the monster beat me. I sought out
2010 Hrothgar, first, came to him in his hall;
When Healfdane's famous son heard
That I'd come to challenge Grendel, he gave me
A seat of honor alongside his son.
His followers were drinking; I joined their feast,
2015 Sat with that band, as bright and loud-tongued
As any I've ever seen. His famous
Queen went back and forth, hurrying
The cup-bearing boys, giving bracelets
And rings to her husband's warriors. I heard
2020 The oldest soldiers of all calling
For ale from Hrothgar's daughter's hands,

And Freaw was the way they greeted her when she gave them
The golden cups. And Hrothgar will give her
To Ingeld, gracious Froda's son;
She and that ripening soldier will be married, 2025
The Danes' great lord and protector has declared,
Hoping that his quarrel with the Hathobards can be settled
By a woman. He's wrong: how many wars
Have been put to rest in a prince's bed?
Few. A bride can bring a little 2030
Peace, make spears silent for a time,
But not long. Ingeld and all his men
Will be drinking in the hall, when the wedding is done
And Freaw is his wife; the Danes will be wearing
Gleaming armor and ring-marked old swords; 2035
And the prince and his people will remember those treasures,
Will remember that their fathers once wore them, fell
With those helmets on their heads, those swords in their hands.

29

"And seeing their ancestral armor and weapons
Ingeld and his followers will be angry. And one
Of his soldiers, sitting with ale in his cup
And bitterness heavy in his heart, will remember
War and death, and while he sits and drinks
His sharp old tongue will begin to tempt
Some younger warrior, pushing and probing
For a new war:

"'That sword, that precious old blade
Over there, I think you know it, friend.
Your father carried it, fought with it the last time
He could swing a sword; the Danes killed him
—And many more of our men—and stripped
The dead bodies: the brave, bold Danes!
One of the princess' people, here,
Now, might be the murderer's son,
Boasting about his treasures, his ancient
Armor—which ought to be yours, by right.'

"Bitter words will work in a hot-tempered
Brain, pushing up thoughts of the past,
And then, when he can, calling his father's
Name, the youngster will kill some innocent
Dane, a servant—and bloody sword
In hand will run from the hall, knowing
His way through the woods. But war will begin

Beowulf

As he runs, to the sound of broken oaths,
And its heat will dry up Ingeld's heart, 2065
Leave him indifferent to his Danish bride.
Hrothgar may think the Hathobards love him,
Loving Freaw, but the friendship can't last,
The vows are worthless.
                "But of Grendel: you need to 2070
Know more to know everything; I ought to
Go on. It was early in the evening, Heaven's
Jewel had slid to its rest, and the jealous
Monster, planning murder, came seeking us
Out, stalking us as we guarded Hrothgar's 2075
Hall. Hondshew, sleeping in his armor,
Was the first Geat he reached: Grendel
Seized him, tore him apart, swallowed him
Down, feet and all, as fate
Had decreed—a glorious young soldier, killed 2080
In his prime. Yet Grendel had only begun
His bloody work, meant to leave us
With his belly and his pouch both full, and Herot
Half-empty. Then he tested his strength against mine,
Hand to hand. His pouch hung 2085
At his side, a huge bag sewn
From a dragon's skin, worked with a devil's
Skill; it was closed by a marvelous clasp.
The monster intended to take me, put me
Inside, save me for another meal. 2090
He was bold and strong, but once I stood
On my feet his strength was useless, and it failed him.

30

"The whole tale of how I killed him,
Repaid him in kind for all the evil
2095 He'd done, would take too long: your people,
My prince, were honored in the doing. He escaped,
Found a few minutes of life, but his hand,
His whole right arm, stayed in Herot;
The miserable creature crept away,
2100 Dropped to the bottom of his lake, half dead
As he fell. When the sun had returned, the Danes'
Great king poured out treasure, repaid me
In hammered gold for the bloody battle
I'd fought in his name. He ordered a feast;
There were songs, and the telling of tales. One
2105   ancient
Dane told of long-dead times,
And sometimes Hrothgar himself, with the harp
In his lap, stroked its silvery strings
And told wonderful stories, a brave king
2110 Reciting unhappy truths about good
And evil—and sometimes he wove his stories
On the mournful thread of old age, remembering
Buried strength and the battles it had won.
He would weep, the old king, wise with many
2115 Winters, remembering what he'd done, once,
What he'd seen, what he knew. And so we sat
The day away, feasting. Then darkness

Fell again, and Grendel's mother
Was waiting, ready for revenge, hating
The Danes for her son's death. The monstrous
Hag succeeded, burst boldly into Herot
And killed Esher, one of the king's oldest
And wisest soldiers. But when the sun shone
Once more the death-weary Danes could not build
A pyre and burn his belovèd body,
Lay him on flaming logs, return ashes
To dust: she'd carried away his corpse,
Brought it to her den deep in the water.
Hrothgar had wept for many of his men,
But this time his heart melted, this
Was the worst. He begged me, in your name, half-
    weeping
As he spoke, to seek still greater glory
Deep in the swirling waves, to win
Still higher fame, and the gifts he would give me.
Down in that surging lake I sought
And found her, the horrible hag, fierce
And wild; we fought, clutching and grasping;
The water ran red with blood and at last,
With a mighty sword that had hung on the wall,
I cut off her head. I had barely escaped
With my life, my death was not written. And the
    Danes'
Protector, Healfdane's great son, heaped up
Treasures and precious jewels to reward me.

31

"He lived his life as a good king must:
I lost nothing, none of the gifts
My strength could have earned me. He opened his store
Of gems and armor, let me choose as I liked,
So I could bring his riches to you, my ruler,
And prove his friendship, and my love. Your favor
Still governs my life: I have almost no family,
Higlac, almost no one, now, but you."
  Then Beowulf ordered them to bring in the boar-head
Banner, the towering helmet, the ancient,
Silvery armor, and the gold-carved sword:
  "This war-gear was Hrothgar's reward, my gift
From his wise old hands. He wanted me to tell you,
First, whose treasures these were. Hergar
Had owned them, his older brother, who was king
Of Denmark until death gave Hrothgar the throne:
But Hergar kept them, would not give them to Herward,
His brave young son, though the boy had proved
His loyalty. These are yours: may they serve you well!"
  And after the gleaming armor four horses
Were led in, four bays, swift and all
Alike. Beowulf had brought his king

Horses and treasure—as a man must,
Not weaving nets of malice for his comrades,
Preparing their death in the dark, with secret,
Cunning tricks. Higlac trusted
His nephew, leaned on his strength, in war, 2170
Each of them intent on the other's joy.
And Beowulf gave Welthow's gift, her wonderful
Necklace, to Higd, Higlac's queen,
And gave her, also, three supple, graceful,
Saddle-bright horses; she received his presents, 2175
Then wore that wonderful jewel on her breast.
  So Edgetho's son proved himself,
Did as a famous soldier must do
If glory is what he seeks: not killing his comrades
In drunken rages, his heart not savage, 2180
But guarding God's gracious gift, his strength,
Using it only in war, and then using it
Bravely. And yet as a boy he was scorned:
The Geats considered him worthless. When he sat
In their mead-hall, and their lord was making men rich, 2185
He held no claim on the king's good will.
They were sure he was lazy, noble but slow.
The world spun round, he was a warrior more famous
Than any, and all the insults were wiped out.
  Then Higlac, protector of his people, brought in 2190
His father's—Beowulf's grandfather's—great sword,
Worked in gold; none of the Geats
Could boast of a better weapon. He laid it
In Beowulf's lap, then gave him seven
Thousand hides of land, houses 2195
And ground and all. Geatland was home
For both king and prince; their fathers had left them
Buildings and fields—but Higlac's inheritance
Stretched further, it was he who was king, and was followed.

* * *

2200 Afterwards, in the time when Higlac was dead
And Herdred, his son, who'd ruled the Geats
After his father, had followed him into darkness—
Killed in battle with the Swedes, who smashed
His shield, cut through the soldiers surrounding
2205 Their king—then, when Higd's one son
Was gone, Beowulf ruled in Geatland,
Took the throne he'd refused, once,
And held it long and well. He was old
With years and wisdom, fifty winters
2210 A king, when a dragon awoke from its darkness
And dreams and brought terror to his people.
 The beast
Had slept in a huge stone tower, with a hidden
Path beneath; a man stumbled on
The entrance, went in, discovered the ancient
2215 Treasure, the pagan jewels and gold
The dragon had been guarding, and dazzled and
 greedy
Stole a gem-studded cup, and fled.
But now the dragon hid nothing, neither
The theft nor itself; it swept through the darkness,
2220 And all Geatland knew its anger.

32

But the thief had not come to steal; he stole,
And roused the dragon, not from desire
But need. He was someone's slave, had been beaten
By his masters, had run from all men's sight,
But with no place to hide; then he found the hidden   2225
Path, and used it. And once inside,
Seeing the sleeping beast, staring as it
Yawned and stretched, not wanting to wake it,
Terror-struck, he turned and ran for his life,
Taking the jeweled cup.   2230
                  That tower
Was heaped high with hidden treasure, stored there
Years before by the last survivor
Of a noble race, ancient riches
Left in the darkness as the end of a dynasty   2235
Came. Death had taken them, one
By one, and the warrior who watched over all
That remained mourned their fate, expecting,
Soon, the same for himself, knowing
The gold and jewels he had guarded so long   2240
Could not bring him pleasure much longer. He
    brought
The precious cups, the armor and the ancient
Swords, to a stone tower built
Near the sea, below a cliff, a sealed
Fortress with no windows, no doors, waves   2245

In front of it, rocks behind. Then he spoke:
"Take these treasures, earth, now that no one
Living can enjoy them. They were yours, in the
   beginning;
Allow them to return. War and terror
Have swept away my people, shut
Their eyes to delight and to living, closed
The door to all gladness. No one is left
To lift these swords, polish these jeweled
Cups: no one leads, no one follows. These hammered
Helmets, worked with gold, will tarnish
And crack; the hands that should clean and polish them
Are still forever. And these mail shirts, worn
In battle, once, while swords crashed
And blades bit into shields and men,
Will rust away like the warriors who owned them.
None of these treasures will travel to distant
Lands, following their lords. The harp's
Bright song, the hawk crossing through the hall
On its swift wings, the stallion tramping
In the courtyard—all gone, creatures of every
Kind, and their masters, hurled to the grave!"
   And so he spoke, sadly, of those
Long dead, and lived from day to day,
Joyless, until, at last, death touched
His heart and took him, too. And a stalker
In the night, a flaming dragon, found
The treasure unguarded; he whom men fear
Came flying through the darkness, wrapped in fire,
Seeking caves and stone-split ruins
But finding gold. Then it stayed, buried
Itself with heathen silver and jewels
It could neither use nor ever abandon.
   So mankind's enemy, the mighty beast,
Slept in those stone walls for hundreds
Of years; a runaway slave roused it,

Stole a jeweled cup and bought
His master's forgiveness, begged for mercy
And was pardoned when his delighted lord took
    the present
He bore, turned it in his hands and stared
At the ancient carvings. The cup brought peace   2285
To a slave, pleased his master, but stirred
A dragon's anger. It turned, hunting
The thief's tracks, and found them, saw
Where its visitor had come and gone. He'd survived,
Had come close enough to touch its scaly   2290
Head and yet lived, as it lifted its cavernous
Jaws, through the grace of almighty God
And a pair of quiet, quick-moving feet.
The dragon followed his steps, anxious
To find the man who had robbed it of silver   2295
And sleep; it circled around and around
The tower, determined to catch him, but could not,
He had run too fast, the wilderness was empty.
The beast went back to its treasure, planning
A bloody revenge, and found what was missing,   2300
Saw what thieving hands had stolen.
Then it crouched on the stones, counting off
The hours till the Almighty's candle went out,
And evening came, and wild with anger
It could fly burning across the land, killing   2305
And destroying with its breath. Then the sun was
    gone,
And its heart was glad: glowing with rage
It left the tower, impatient to repay
Its enemies. The people suffered, everyone
Lived in terror, but when Beowulf had learned   2310
Of their trouble his fate was worse, and came
    quickly.

33

    Vomiting fire and smoke, the dragon
Burned down their homes. They watched in horror
As the flames rose up: the angry monster
2315 Meant to leave nothing alive. And the signs
Of its anger flickered and glowed in the darkness,
Visible for miles, tokens of its hate
And its cruelty, spread like a warning to the Geats
Who had broken its rest. Then it hurried back
2320 To its tower, to its hidden treasure, before dawn
Could come. It had wrapped its flames around
The Geats; now it trusted in stone
Walls, and its strength, to protect it. But they would not.
    Then they came to Beowulf, their king, and announced
2325 That his hall, his throne, the best of buildings,
Had melted away in the dragon's burning
Breath. Their words brought misery, Beowulf's
Sorrow beat at his heart: he accused
Himself of breaking God's law, of bringing
2330 The Almighty's anger down on his people.
Reproach pounded in his breast, gloomy
And dark, and the world seemed a different place.
But the hall was gone, the dragon's molten
Breath had licked across it, burned it
2335 To ashes, near the shore it had guarded. The Geats

Deserved revenge; Beowulf, their leader
And lord, began to plan it, ordered
A battle-shield shaped of iron, knowing that
Wood would be useless, that no linden shield
Could help him, protect him, in the flaming heat 2340
Of the beast's breath. That noble prince
Would end his days on earth, soon,
Would leave this brief life, but would take the dragon
With him, tear it from the heaped-up treasure
It had guarded so long. And he'd go to it alone, 2345
Scorning to lead soldiers against such
An enemy: he saw nothing to fear, thought nothing
Of the beast's claws, or wings, or flaming
Jaws—he had fought, before, against worse
Odds, had survived, been victorious, in harsher 2350
Battles, beginning in Herot, Hrothgar's
Unlucky hall. He'd killed Grendel
And his mother, swept that murdering tribe
Away. And he'd fought in Higlac's war
With the Frisians, fought at his lord's side 2355
Till a sword reached out and drank Higlac's
Blood, till a blade swung in the rush
Of battle killed the Geats' great king.
Then Beowulf escaped, broke through Frisian
Shields and swam to freedom, saving 2360
Thirty sets of armor from the scavenging
Franks, river people who robbed
The dead as they floated by. Beowulf
Offered them only his sword, ended
So many jackal lives that the few 2365
Who were able skulked silently home, glad
To leave him. So Beowulf swam sadly back
To Geatland, almost the only survivor
Of a foolish war. Higlac's widow
Brought him the crown, offered him the kingdom, 2370
Not trusting Herdred, her son and Higlac's,
To beat off foreign invaders. But Beowulf

Refused to rule when his lord's own son
Was alive, and the leaderless Geats could choose
2375 A rightful king. He gave Herdred
All his support, offering an open
Heart where Higlac's young son could see
Wisdom he still lacked himself: warmth
And good will were what Beowulf brought his new king.
2380 But Swedish exiles came, seeking
Protection; they were rebels against Onela,
Healfdane's son-in-law and the best ring-giver
His people had ever known. And Onela
Came, too, a mighty king, marched
2385 On Geatland with a huge army; Herdred
Had given his word and now he gave
His life, shielding the Swedish strangers.
Onela wanted nothing more:
When Herdred had fallen that famous warrior
2390 Went back to Sweden, let Beowulf rule!

34

But Beowulf remembered how his king had
   been killed.
As soon as he could he lent the last
Of the Swedish rebels soldiers and gold,
Helped him to a bitter battle across
The wide sea, where victory, and revenge, and the
   Swedish   2395
Throne were won, and Onela was slain.
   So Edgetho's son survived, no matter
What dangers he met, what battles he fought,
Brave and forever triumphant, till the day
Fate sent him to the dragon and sent him death.   2400
A dozen warriors walked with their angry
King, when he was brought to the beast; Beowulf
Knew, by then, what had woken the monster,
And enraged it. The cup had come to him, traveled
From dragon to slave, to master, to king,   2405
And the slave was their guide, had begun the Geats'
Affliction, and now, afraid of both beast
And men, was forced to lead them to the monster's
Hidden home. He showed them the huge
Stones, set deep in the ground, with the sea   2410
Beating on the rocks close by. Beowulf
Stared, listening to stories of the gold
And riches heaped inside. Hidden,
But wakeful, now, the dragon waited,

100   *Beowulf*

₂₄₁₅ Ready to greet him. Gold and hammered
Armor have been buried in pleasanter places!
  The battle-brave king rested on the shore,
While his soldiers wished him well, urged him
On. But Beowulf's heart was heavy:
₂₄₂₀ His soul sensed how close fate
Had come, felt something, not fear but knowledge
Of old age. His armor was strong, but his arm
Hung like his heart. Body and soul
Might part, here; his blood might be spilled,
₂₄₂₅ His spirit torn from his flesh. Then he spoke.
  "My early days were full of war,
And I survived it all; I can remember everything.
I was seven years old when Hrethel opened
His home and his heart for me, when my king and lord
₂₄₃₀ Took me from my father and kept me, taught me,
Gave me gold and pleasure, glad that I sat
At his knee. And he never loved me less
Than any of his sons—Herbald, the oldest
Of all, or Hathcyn, or Higlac, my lord.
₂₄₃₅ Herbald died a horrible death,
Killed while hunting: Hathcyn, his brother,
Stretched his horn-tipped bow, sent
An arrow flying, but missed his mark
And hit Herbald instead, found him
₂₄₄₀ With a bloody point and pierced him through.
The crime was great, the guilt was plain,
But nothing could be done, no vengeance, no death
To repay that death, no punishment, nothing.
  "So with the graybeard whose son sins
₂₄₄₅ Against the king, and is hanged: he stands
Watching his child swing on the gallows,
Lamenting, helpless, while his flesh and blood
Hangs for the raven to pluck. He can raise
His voice in sorrow, but revenge is impossible.
₂₄₅₀ And every morning he remembers how his son
Died, and despairs; no son to come

Matters, no future heir, to a father
Forced to live through such misery. The place
Where his son once dwelled, before death compelled him
To journey away, is a windy wasteland, 2455
Empty, cheerless; the childless father
Shudders, seeing it. So riders and ridden
Sleep in the ground; pleasure is gone,
The harp is silent, and hope is forgotten.

35

"And then, crying his sorrow, he crawls
To his bed: the world, and his home, hurt him
With their emptiness. And so it seemed to Hrethel,
When Herbald was dead, and his heart swelled
With grief. The murderer lived; he felt
No love for him, now, but nothing could help,
Word nor hand nor sharp-honed blade,
War nor hate, battle or blood
Or law. The pain could find no relief.
He could only live with it, or leave grief and life
Together. When he'd gone to his grave Hathcyn
And Higlac, his sons, inherited everything.

"And then there was war between Geats and Swedes,
Bitter battles carried across
The broad sea, when the mighty Hrethel slept
And Ongentho's sons thought Sweden could safely
Attack, saw no use to pretending friendship
But raided and burned, and near old Rennsburg
Slaughtered Geats with their thieving swords.
My people repaid them, death for death,
Battle for battle, though one of the brothers
Bought that revenge with his life—Hathcyn,
King of the Geats, killed by a Swedish
Sword. But when dawn came the slayer
Was slain, and Higlac's soldiers avenged

Beowulf

Everything with the edge of their blades. Efor 2485
Caught the Swedish king, cracked
His helmet, split his skull, dropped him,
Pale and bleeding, to the ground, then put him
To death with a swift stroke, shouting
His joy. 2490
       "The gifts that Higlac gave me,
And the land, I earned with my sword, as fate
Allowed: he never needed Danes
Or Goths or Swedes, soldiers and allies
Bought with gold, bribed to his side. 2495
My sword was better, and always his.
In every battle my place was in front,
Alone, and so it shall be forever,
As long as this sword lasts, serves me
In the future as it has served me before. So 2500
I killed Dagref, the Frank, who brought death
To Higlac, and who looted his corpse: Higd's
Necklace, Welthow's treasure, never
Came to Dagref's king. The thief
Fell in battle, but not on my blade. 2505
He was brave and strong, but I swept him in my arms,
Ground him against me till his bones broke,
Till his blood burst out. And now I shall fight
For this treasure, fight with both hand and sword."
    And Beowulf uttered his final boast: 2510
  "I've never known fear; as a youth I fought
In endless battles. I am old, now,
But I will fight again, seek fame still,
If the dragon hiding in his tower dares
To face me." 2515
        Then he said farewell to his followers,
Each in his turn, for the last time:
  "I'd use no sword, no weapon, if this beast
Could be killed without it, crushed to death
Like Grendel, gripped in my hands and torn 2520
Limb from limb. But his breath will be burning

Hot, poison will pour from his tongue.
I feel no shame, with shield and sword
And armor, against this monster: when he comes to me
2525 I mean to stand, not run from his shooting
Flames, stand till fate decides
Which of us wins. My heart is firm,
My hands calm: I need no hot
Words. Wait for me close by, my friends.
2530 We shall see, soon, who will survive
This bloody battle, stand when the fighting
Is done. No one else could do
What I mean to, here, no man but me
Could hope to defeat this monster. No one
2535 Could try. And this dragon's treasure, his gold
And everything hidden in that tower, will be mine
Or war will sweep me to a bitter death!"
    Then Beowulf rose, still brave, still strong,
And with his shield at his side, and a mail shirt on his breast,
2540 Strode calmly, confidently, toward the tower, under
The rocky cliffs: no coward could have walked there!
And then he who'd endured dozens of desperate
Battles, who'd stood boldly while swords and shields
Clashed, the best of kings, saw
2545 Huge stone arches and felt the heat
Of the dragon's breath, flooding down
Through the hidden entrance, too hot for anyone
To stand, a streaming current of fire
And smoke that blocked all passage. And the Geats'
2550 Lord and leader, angry, lowered
His sword and roared out a battle cry,
A call so loud and clear that it reached through
The hoary rock, hung in the dragon's
Ear. The beast rose, angry,

Knowing a man had come—and then nothing 2555
But war could have followed. Its breath came first,
A steaming cloud pouring from the stone.
Then the earth itself shook. Beowulf
Swung his shield into place, held it
In front of him, facing the entrance. The dragon 2560
Coiled and uncoiled, its heart urging it
Into battle. Beowulf's ancient sword
Was waiting, unsheathed, his sharp and gleaming
Blade. The beast came closer; both of them
Were ready, each set on slaughter. The Geats' 2565
Great prince stood firm, unmoving, prepared
Behind his high shield, waiting in his shining
Armor. The monster came quickly toward him,
Pouring out fire and smoke, hurrying
To its fate. Flames beat at the iron 2570
Shield, and for a time it held, protected
Beowulf as he'd planned; then it began to melt,
And for the first time in his life that famous prince
Fought with fate against him, with glory
Denied him. He knew it, but he raised his sword 2575
And struck at the dragon's scaly hide.
The ancient blade broke, bit into
The monster's skin, drew blood, but cracked
And failed him before it went deep enough, helped him
Less than he needed. The dragon leaped 2580
With pain, thrashed and beat at him, spouting
Murderous flames, spreading them everywhere.
And the Geats' ring-giver did not boast of glorious
Victories in other wars: his weapon
Had failed him, deserted him, now when he needed it 2585
Most, that excellent sword. Edgetho's
Famous son stared at death,
Unwilling to leave this world, to exchange it
For a dwelling in some distant place—a journey
Into darkness that all men must make, as death 2590

Ends their few brief hours on earth.
    Quickly, the dragon came at him, encouraged
As Beowulf fell back; its breath flared,
And he suffered, wrapped around in swirling
2595 Flames—a king, before, but now
A beaten warrior. None of his comrades
Came to him, helped him, his brave and noble
Followers; they ran for their lives, fled
Deep in a wood. And only one of them
2600 Remained, stood there, miserable, remembering,
As a good man must, what kinship should mean.

36

His name was Wiglaf, he was Wexstan's son
And a good soldier; his family had been Swedish,
Once. Watching Beowulf, he could see
How his king was suffering, burning. Remembering
Everything his lord and cousin had given him,
Armor and gold and the great estates
Wexstan's family enjoyed, Wiglaf's
Mind was made up; he raised his yellow
Shield and drew his sword—an ancient
Weapon that had once belonged to Onela's
Nephew, and that Wexstan had won, killing
The prince when he fled from Sweden, sought safety
With Herdred, and found death. And Wiglaf's father
Had carried the dead man's armor, and his sword,
To Onela, and the king had said nothing, only
Given him armor and sword and all,
Everything his rebel nephew had owned
And lost when he left this life. And Wexstan
Had kept those shining gifts, held them
For years, waiting for his son to use them,
Wear them as honorably and well as once
His father had done; then Wexstan died
And Wiglaf was his heir, inherited treasures
And weapons and land. He'd never worn

That armor, fought with that sword, until Beowulf
Called him to his side, led him into war.
But his soul did not melt, his sword was strong;
The dragon discovered his courage, and his weapon,
2630 When the rush of battle brought them together.
    And Wiglaf, his heart heavy, uttered
The kind of words his comrades deserved:
    "I remember how we sat in the mead-hall, drinking
And boasting of how brave we'd be when Beowulf
2635 Needed us, he who gave us these swords
And armor: all of us swore to repay him,
When the time came, kindness for kindness
—With our lives, if he needed them. He allowed us to join him,
Chose us from all his great army, thinking
2640 Our boasting words had some weight, believing
Our promises, trusting our swords. He took us
For soldiers, for men. He meant to kill
This monster himself, our mighty king,
Fight this battle alone and unaided,
2645 As in the days when his strength and daring dazzled
Men's eyes. But those days are over and gone
And now our lord must lean on younger
Arms. And we must go to him, while angry
Flames burn at his flesh, help
2650 Our glorious king! By almighty God,
I'd rather burn myself than see
Flames swirling around my lord.
And who are we to carry home
Our shields before we've slain his enemy
2655 And ours, to run back to our homes with Beowulf
So hard-pressed here? I swear that nothing
He ever did deserved an end
Like this, dying miserably and alone,
Butchered by this savage beast: we swore
2660 That these swords and armor were each for us all!"
    Then he ran to his king, crying encouragement

Beowulf

As he dove through the dragon's deadly fumes:
   "Belovèd Beowulf, remember how you boasted,
Once, that nothing in the world would ever
Destroy your fame: fight to keep it, 2665
Now, be strong and brave, my noble
King, protecting life and fame
Together. My sword will fight at your side!"
   The dragon heard him, the man-hating monster,
And was angry; shining with surging flames 2670
It came for him, anxious to return his visit.
Waves of fire swept at his shield
And the edge began to burn. His mail shirt
Could not help him, but before his hands dropped
The blazing wood Wiglaf jumped 2675
Behind Beowulf's shield; his own was burned
To ashes. Then the famous old hero, remembering
Days of glory, lifted what was left
Of Nagling, his ancient sword, and swung it
With all his strength, smashed the gray 2680
Blade into the beast's head. But then Nagling
Broke to pieces, as iron always
Had in Beowulf's hands. His arms
Were too strong, the hardest blade could not help him,
The most wonderfully worked. He carried them to war 2685
But fate had decreed that the Geats' great king
Would be no better for any weapon.
   Then the monster charged again, vomiting
Fire, wild with pain, rushed out
Fierce and dreadful, its fear forgotten. 2690
Watching for its chance it drove its tusks
Into Beowulf's neck; he staggered, the blood
Came flooding forth, fell like rain.

37

    And then when Beowulf needed him most
2695 Wiglaf showed his courage, his strength
And skill, and the boldness he was born with.
    Ignoring
The dragon's head, he helped his lord
By striking lower down. The sword
Sank in; his hand was burned, but the shining
2700 Blade had done its work, the dragon's
Belching flames began to flicker
And die away. And Beowulf drew
His battle-sharp dagger: the bloodstained old king
Still knew what he was doing. Quickly, he cut
2705 The beast in half, slit it apart.
It fell, their courage had killed it, two noble
Cousins had joined in the dragon's death.
Yet what they did all men must do
When the time comes! But the triumph was the last
2710 Beowulf would ever earn, the end
Of greatness and life together. The wound
In his neck began to swell and grow;
He could feel something stirring, burning
In his veins, a stinging venom, and knew
2715 The beast's fangs had left it. He fumbled
Along the wall, found a slab
Of stone, and dropped down; above him he saw
Huge stone arches and heavy posts,

110

Holding up the roof of that giant hall.
Then Wiglaf's gentle hands bathed 2720
The bloodstained prince, his glorious lord,
Weary of war, and loosened his helmet.

   Beowulf spoke, in spite of the swollen,
Livid wound, knowing he'd unwound
His string of days on earth, seen 2725
As much as God would grant him; all worldly
Pleasure was gone, as life would go,
Soon:

   "I'd leave my armor to my son,
Now, if God had given me an heir, 2730
A child born of my body, his life
Created from mine. I've worn this crown
For fifty winters: no neighboring people
Have tried to threaten the Geats, sent soldiers
Against us or talked of terror. My days 2735
Have gone by as fate willed, waiting
For its word to be spoken, ruling as well
As I knew how, swearing no unholy oaths,
Seeking no lying wars. I can leave
This life happy; I can die, here, 2740
Knowing the Lord of all life has never
Watched me wash my sword in blood
Born of my own family. Belovèd
Wiglaf, go, quickly, find
The dragon's treasure: we've taken its life, 2745
But its gold is ours, too. Hurry,
Bring me ancient silver, precious
Jewels, shining armor and gems,
Before I die. Death will be softer,
Leaving life and this people I've ruled 2750
So long, if I look at this last of all prizes."

38

Then Wexstan's son went in, as quickly
As he could, did as the dying Beowulf
Asked, entered the inner darkness
Of the tower, went with his mail shirt and his
2755   sword.
Flushed with victory he groped his way,
A brave young warrior, and suddenly saw
Piles of gleaming gold, precious
Gems, scattered on the floor, cups
2760 And bracelets, rusty old helmets, beautifully
Made but rotting with no hands to rub
And polish them. They lay where the dragon left them;
It had flown in the darkness, once, before fighting
Its final battle. (So gold can easily
2765 Triumph, defeat the strongest of men,
No matter how deep it is hidden!) And he saw,
Hanging high above, a golden
Banner, woven by the best of weavers
And beautiful. And over everything he saw
2770 A strange light, shining everywhere,
On walls and floor and treasure. Nothing
Moved, no other monsters appeared;
He took what he wanted, all the treasures
That pleased his eye, heavy plates
2775 And golden cups and the glorious banner,

Loaded his arms with all they could hold.
Beowulf's dagger, his iron blade,
Had finished the fire-spitting terror
That once protected tower and treasures
Alike; the gray-bearded lord of the Geats 2780
Had ended those flying, burning raids
Forever.
      Then Wiglaf went back, anxious
To return while Beowulf was alive, to bring him
Treasure they'd won together. He ran, 2785
Hoping his wounded king, weak
And dying, had not left the world too soon.
Then he brought their treasure to Beowulf, and found
His famous king bloody, gasping
For breath. But Wiglaf sprinkled water 2790
Over his lord, until the words
Deep in his breast broke through and were heard.
Beholding the treasure he spoke, haltingly:
  "For this, this gold, these jewels, I thank
Our Father in Heaven, Ruler of the Earth— 2795
For all of this, that His grace has given me,
Allowed me to bring to my people while breath
Still came to my lips. I sold my life
For this treasure, and I sold it well. Take
What I leave, Wiglaf, lead my people, 2800
Help them; my time is gone. Have
The brave Geats build me a tomb,
When the funeral flames have burned me, and build it
Here, at the water's edge, high
On this spit of land, so sailors can see 2805
This tower, and remember my name, and call it
Beowulf's tower, and boats in the darkness
And mist, crossing the sea, will know it."
  Then that brave king gave the golden
Necklace from around his throat to Wiglaf, 2810
Gave him his gold-covered helmet, and his rings,

And his mail shirt, and ordered him to use them well:
"You're the last of all our far-flung family.
Fate has swept our race away,
2815 Taken warriors in their strength and led them
To the death that was waiting. And now I follow them."
The old man's mouth was silent, spoke
No more, had said as much as it could;
He would sleep in the fire, soon. His soul
2820 Left his flesh, flew to glory.

39

And then Wiglaf was left, a young warrior
Sadly watching his belovèd king,
Seeing him stretched on the ground, left guarding
A torn and bloody corpse. But Beowulf's
Killer was dead, too, the coiled   2825
Dragon, cut in half, cold
And motionless: men, and their swords, had swept it
From the earth, left it lying in front of
Its tower, won its treasure when it fell
Crashing to the ground, cut it apart   2830
With their hammered blades, driven them deep in
Its belly. It would never fly through the night,
Glowing in the dark sky, glorying
In its riches, burning and raiding: two warriors
Had shown it their strength, slain it with their
    swords.   2835
Not many men, no matter how strong,
No matter how daring, how bold, had done
As well, rushing at its venomous fangs,
Or even quietly entering its tower,
Intending to steal but finding the treasure's   2840
Guardian awake, watching and ready
To greet them. Beowulf had gotten its gold,
Bought it with blood; dragon and king
Had ended each other's days on earth.

And when the battle was over Beowulf's followers
2845 Came out of the wood, cowards and traitors,
Knowing the dragon was dead. Afraid,
While it spit its fires, to fight in their lord's
Defense, to throw their javelins and spears,
2850 They came like shamefaced jackals, their shields
In their hands, to the place where the prince lay dead,
And waited for Wiglaf to speak. He was sitting
Near Beowulf's body, wearily sprinkling
Water in the dead man's face, trying
2855 To stir him. He could not. No one could have kept
Life in their lord's body, or turned
Aside the Lord's will: world
And men and all move as He orders,
And always have, and always will.
2860 Then Wiglaf turned and angrily told them
What men without courage must hear.
Wexstan's brave son stared at the traitors,
His heart sorrowful, and said what he had to:
"I say what anyone who speaks the truth
2865 Must say. Your lord gave you gifts,
Swords and the armor you stand in now;
You sat on the mead-hall benches, prince
And followers, and he gave you, with open hands,
Helmets and mail shirts, hunted across
2870 The world for the best of weapons. War
Came and you ran like cowards, dropped
Your swords as soon as the danger was real.
Should Beowulf have boasted of your help, rejoiced
In your loyal strength? With God's good grace
2875 He helped himself, swung his sword
Alone, won his own revenge.
The help I gave him was nothing, but all
I was able to give; I went to him, knowing
That nothing but Beowulf's strength could save us,

And my sword was lucky, found some vital 2880
Place and bled the burning flames
Away. Too few of his warriors remembered
To come, when our lord faced death, alone.
And now the giving of swords, of golden
Rings and rich estates, is over, 2885
Ended for you and everyone who shares
Your blood: when the brave Geats hear
How you bolted and ran none of your race
Will have anything left but their lives. And death
Would be better for them all, and for you, than the kind 2890
Of life you can lead, branded with disgrace!"

He's angry w/ them

40

    Then Wiglaf ordered a messenger to ride
Across the cliff, to the Geats who'd waited
The morning away, sadly wondering
2895 If their belovèd king would return, or be killed,
A troop of soldiers sitting in silence
And hoping for the best. Whipping his horse
The herald came to them; they crowded around,
And he told them everything, present and past:
2900   "Our lord is dead, leader of this people.
The dragon killed him, but the beast is dead,
Too, cut in half by a dagger;
Beowulf's enemy sleeps in its blood.
No sword could pierce its skin, wound
2905 That monster. Wiglaf is sitting in mourning,
Close to Beowulf's body, Wexstan's
Weary son, silent and sad,
Keeping watch for our king, there
Where Beowulf and the beast that killed him lie dead.
2910   "And this people can expect fighting, once
The Franks, and the Frisians, have heard that our king
Lies dead. The news will spread quickly.
Higlac began our bitter quarrel
With the Franks, raiding along their river
2915 Rhine with ships and soldiers, until

118

They attacked him with a huge army, and Higlac
Was killed, the king and many of our men,
Mailed warriors defeated in war,
Beaten by numbers. He brought no treasure
To the mead-hall, after that battle. And ever 2920
After we knew no friendship with the Franks.
    "Nor can we expect peace from the Swedes.
Everyone knows how their old king,
Ongentho, killed Hathcyn, caught him
Near a wood when our young lord went 2925
To war too soon, dared too much.
The wise old Swede, always terrible
In war, allowed the Geats to land
And begin to loot, then broke them with a lightning
Attack, taking back treasure and his kidnaped 2930
Queen, and taking our king's life.
And then he followed his beaten enemies,
Drove them in front of Swedish swords
Until darkness dropped, and weary, lordless,
They could hide in the wood. But he waited, Ongentho 2935
With his mass of soldiers, circled around
The Geats who'd survived, who'd escaped him, calling
Threats and boasts at that wretched band
The whole night through. In the morning he'd hang
A few, he promised, to amuse the birds, 2940
Then slaughter the rest. But the sun rose
To the sound of Higlac's horns and trumpets,
Light and that battle cry coming together
And turning sadhearted Geats into soldiers.
Higlac had followed his people, and found them. 2945

41

"Then blood was everywhere, two bands of Geats
Falling on the Swedes, men fighting
On all sides, butchering each other.
Sadly, Ongentho ordered his soldiers
2950 Back, to the high ground where he'd built
A fortress; he'd heard of Higlac, knew
His boldness and strength. Out in the open
He could never resist such a soldier, defend
Hard-won treasure, Swedish wives
2955 And children, against the Geats' new king.
Brave but wise, he fled, sought safety
Behind earthen walls. Eagerly, the Geats
Followed, sweeping across the field,
Smashing through the walls, waving Higlac's
Banners as they came. Then the gray-haired old
2960 king
Was brought to bay, bright sword-blades
Forcing the lord of the Swedes to take
Judgment at Efor's hands. Efor's
Brother, Wulf, raised his weapon
2965 First, swung it angrily at the fierce
Old king, cracked his helmet; blood
Seeped through his hair. But the brave old Swede
Felt no fear: he quickly returned
A better blow than he'd gotten, faced

Toward Wulf and struck him savagely. And Efor's
Bold brother was staggered, half raised his sword
But only dropped it to the ground. Ongentho's
Blade had cut through his helmet, his head
Spouted blood, and slowly he fell.
The wound was deep, but death was not due
So soon; fate let him recover, live
On. But Efor, his brave brother,
Seeing Wulf fall, came forward with his broad-bladed
Sword, hammered by giants, and swung it
So hard that Ongentho's shield shattered
And he sank to the earth, his life ended.
Then, with the battlefield theirs, the Geats
Rushed to Wulf's side, raised him up
And bound his wound. Wulf's brother
Stripped the old Swede, took
His iron mail shirt, his hilted sword
And his helmet, and all his ancient war-gear,
And brought them to Higlac, his new lord.
The king welcomed him, warmly thanked him
For his gifts and promised, there where everyone
Could hear, that as soon as he sat in his mead-hall
Again Efor and Wulf would have treasure
Heaped in their battle-hard hands; he'd repay them
Their bravery with wealth, give them gold
And lands and silver rings, rich rewards for the glorious
Deeds they'd done with their swords. The Geats agreed. And to prove
Efor's grace in his eyes, Higlac
Swore he'd give him his only daughter.

"These are the quarrels, the hatreds, the feuds,
That will bring us battles, force us into war
With the Swedes, as soon as they've learned how our lord
Is dead, know that the Geats are leaderless,
Have lost the best of kings, Beowulf—

                He who held our enemies away,
 3005   Kept land and treasure intact, who saved
        Hrothgar and the Danes—he who lived
        All his long life bravely. Then let us
        Go to him, hurry to our glorious lord,
        Behold him lifeless, and quickly carry him
 3010   To the flames. The fire must melt more
        Than his bones, more than his share of treasure:
        Give it all of this golden pile,
        This terrible, uncounted heap of cups
        And rings, bought with his blood. Burn it
 3015   To ashes, to nothingness. No one living
        Should enjoy these jewels; no beautiful women
        Wear them, gleaming and golden, from their necks,
        But walk, instead, sad and alone
        In a hundred foreign lands, their laughter
 3020   Gone forever, as Beowulf's has gone,
        His pleasure and his joy. Spears shall be lifted,
        Many cold mornings, lifted and thrown,
        And warriors shall waken to no harp's bright call
        But the croak of the dark-black raven, ready
 3025   To welcome the dead, anxious to tell
        The eagle how he stuffed his craw with corpses,
        Filled his belly even faster than the wolves."
           And so the messenger spoke, a brave
        Man on an ugly errand, telling
 3030   Only the truth. Then the warriors rose,
        Walked slowly down from the cliff, stared
        At those wonderful sights, stood weeping as they saw
        Beowulf dead on the sand, their bold
        Ring-giver resting in his last bed;
 3035   He'd reached the end of his days, their mighty
        War-king, the great lord of the Geats,
        Gone to a glorious death. But they saw
        The dragon first, stretched in front
        Of its tower, a strange, scaly beast
 3040   Gleaming a dozen colors dulled and

Scorched in its own heat. From end
To end fifty feet, it had flown
In the silent darkness, a swift traveler
Tasting the air, then gliding down
To its den. Death held it in his hands;   *3045*
It would guard no caves, no towers, keep
No treasures like the cups, the precious plates
Spread where it lay, silver and brass
Encrusted and rotting, eaten away
As though buried in the earth for a thousand winters.   *3050*
And all this ancient hoard, huge
And golden, was wound around with a spell:
No man could enter the tower, open
Hidden doors, unless the Lord
Of Victories, He who watches over men,   *3055*
Almighty God Himself, was moved
To let him enter, and him alone.

42

    Hiding that treasure deep in its tower,
As the dragon had done, broke God's law
3060 And brought it no good. Guarding its stolen
Wealth it killed Wiglaf's king,
But was punished with death. Who knows when princes
And their soldiers, the bravest and strongest of men,
Are destined to die, their time ended,
3065 Their homes, their halls empty and still?
So Beowulf sought out the dragon, dared it
Into battle, but could never know what God
Had decreed, or that death would come to him, or why.
So the spell was solemnly laid, by men
3070 Long dead; it was meant to last till the day
Of judgment. Whoever stole their jewels,
Their gold, would be cursed with the flames of hell,
Heaped high with sin and guilt, if greed
Was what brought him: God alone could break
3075 Their magic, open His grace to man.
    Then Wiglaf spoke, Wexstan's son:
"How often an entire country suffers
On one man's account! That time has come to us.
We tried to counsel our belovèd king,
3080 Our shield and protection, show him danger,

Urge him to leave the dragon in the dark
Tower it had lain in so long, live there
Till the end of the world. Fate, and his will,
Were too strong. Everyone knows the treasure
His life bought: but Beowulf was worth   *3085*
More than this gold, and the gift is a harsh one.
I've seen it all, been in the tower
Where the jewels and armor were hidden, allowed
To behold them once war and its terror were done.
I gathered them up, gold and silver,   *3090*
Filled my arms as full as I could
And quickly carried them back to my king.
He lay right here, still alive,
Still sure in mind and tongue. He spoke
Sadly, said I should greet you, asked   *3095*
That after you'd burned his body you bring
His ashes here, make this the tallest
Of towers and his tomb—as great and lasting
As his fame, when Beowulf himself walked
The earth and no man living could match him.   *3100*
Come, let us enter the tower, see
The dragon's marvelous treasure one
Last time: I'll lead the way, take you
Close to that heap of curious jewels,
And rings, and gold. Let the pyre be ready   *3105*
And high: as soon as we've seen the dragon's
Hoard we will carry our belovèd king,
Our leader and lord, where he'll lie forever
In God's keeping."
                  Then Wiglaf commanded   *3110*
The wealthiest Geats, brave warriors
And owners of land, leaders of his people,
To bring wood for Beowulf's funeral:
   "Now the fire must feed on his body,
Flames grow heavy and black with him   *3115*
Who endured arrows falling in iron
Showers, feathered shafts, barbed
And sharp, shot through linden shields,

Storms of eager arrowheads dropping."
   And Wexstan's wise son took seven
Of the noblest Geats, led them together
Down the tunnel, deep into the dragon's
Tower; the one in front had a torch,
Held it high in his hands. The best
Of Beowulf's followers entered behind
That gleaming flame: seeing gold
And silver rotting on the ground, with no one
To guard it, the Geats were not troubled with scruples
Or fears, but quickly gathered up
Treasure and carried it out of the tower.
And they rolled the dragon down to the cliff
And dropped it over, let the ocean take it,
The tide sweep it away. Then silver
And gold and precious jewels were put
On a wagon, with Beowulf's body, and brought
Down the jutting sand, where the pyre waited.

43

A huge heap of wood was ready,
Hung around with helmets, and battle
Shields, and shining mail shirts, all
As Beowulf had asked. The bearers brought 3140
Their belovèd lord, their glorious king,
And weeping laid him high on the wood.
Then the warriors began to kindle that greatest
Of funeral fires; smoke rose
Above the flames, black and thick, 3145
And while the wind blew and the fire
Roared they wept, and Beowulf's body
Crumbled and was gone. The Geats stayed,
Moaning their sorrow, lamenting their lord;
A gnarled old woman, hair wound 3150
Tight and gray on her head, groaned
A song of misery, of infinite sadness
And days of mourning, of fear and sorrow
To come, slaughter and terror and captivity.
And Heaven swallowed the billowing smoke. 3155
Then the Geats built the tower, as Beowulf
Had asked, strong and tall, so sailors
Could find it from far and wide; working
For ten long days they made his monument,
Sealed his ashes in walls as straight 3160
And high as wise and willing hands
Could raise them. And the riches he and Wiglaf

Had won from the dragon, rings, necklaces,
Ancient, hammered armor—all
The treasures they'd taken were left there, too,
Silver and jewels buried in the sandy
Ground, back in the earth, again
And forever hidden and useless to men.
And then twelve of the bravest Geats
Rode their horses around the tower,
Telling their sorrow, telling stories
Of their dead king and his greatness, his glory,
Praising him for heroic deeds, for a life
As noble as his name. So should all men
Raise up words for their lords, warm
With love, when their shield and protector leaves
His body behind, sends his soul
On high. And so Beowulf's followers
Rode, mourning their belovèd leader,
Crying that no better king had ever
Lived, no prince so mild, no man
So open to his people, so deserving of praise.

THE END

Glossary of Names

Persons, peoples, and places are here alphabetically arranged according to the form used in this translation. For those familiar with the original, the Old English spelling is also given, in parentheses and italics.

Not all the names mentioned by the poet are here listed. For a variety of esthetic considerations this translation contains a few alternative identifications; there are a few deletions; and for the most part Danes are Danes and Swedes are Swedes, though (for esthetic reasons valid in his language) the poet may describe them as Spear-Danes, Ring-Danes, East-Danes, North-Danes, or West-Danes. No major omissions occur, however, even under the considerable pressure exerted by such as *Ongenþeow, Hygelac,* and *Wealhþeow.*

BEO (*Beowulf*): a Danish king, Shild's son, Healfdane's father. According to Klaeber, "this form of the name is an error for *Bēow.*" To minimize confusion, I have quietly corrected the poet.

BEOWULF (*Beowulf, Biowulf*): possibly mythical son of Edgetho, Higlac's nephew and follower, and later king of the Geats. Following the chronology implicit in the poem, Beowulf was born in A.D. 495, went to Denmark and to Hrothgar's help in 515, accompanied Higlac on his expedition against the Franks and Frisians in 521, became king of the Geats in 533, and died at some indefinite later date. The "fifty years" of his reign are, as Klaeber notes, only "a sort of poetic formula."

BONSTAN (*Beanstan, Banstan, Beahstan*): father of Brecca.

BRECCA (*Breca*): chief of a tribe known as the Brondings; a contemporary and young companion of Beowulf. His father is Bonstan.

BRONDINGS (*Brondingas*): a (Scandinavian?) tribe about whom nothing, including their location, seems to be known.

BROSING (*Brosinga*): possibly a reference to Breisach, on the Rhone near Freiburg; possibly a reference to the Brisings, who made a marvelous necklace for the goddess Freyja (see the Norse Elder Edda).

DAGREF (*Dæghrefn*): a Frank warrior, Higlac's killer, who is killed by Beowulf.

ECLAF (*Ecglaf*): Unferth's father.

EDGETHO (*Ecgþeow*): Beowulf's father, a notable warrior married to Hrethel's one daughter (Beowulf's mother is never named).

EFOR (*Eofor*): a Geat warrior, who kills Ongentho, the Swedish king, and is given Higlac's daughter as a reward.

EMER (*Eomer*): son of Offa.

ERMLAF (*Yrmenlaf*): a Danish nobleman, younger brother of Esher.

ERMRIC (*Eormenric*): a king of the East Goths, historical but converted into the very model of a medieval tyrant; he is so portrayed in the Old English poems "Deor" and "Widsith."

ESHER (*Æschere*): a Danish nobleman, high in the

Glossary of Names

councils of King Hrothgar, and long his close and trusted friend. Esher is killed by Grendel's mother.

FINN (*Finn*): a Frisian king, married to Hnaf's sister.

FITLA (*Fitela*): son (and nephew) of Siegmund. His role, in this and other similar stories, is quite dissimilar to that of Siegfried, who is Siegmund's son (and nephew) in the *Nibelungenlied* and in the Wagner operas.

FRANKS (*Francan*): a West German people, resident near the Rhine and the Meuse rivers. A Frankish tribe conquered Gaul, about A.D. 500, and gave its name to modern France.

FREAW (*Freawaru*): a Danish princess, Hrothgar's daughter. She is given in marriage to Ingeld, a Hathobard prince, in the vain hope of settling the feud between the two peoples.

FRISIANS (*Fresan, Frysan*): a West German people, resident in what is now northwestern Holland.

FRODA (*Froda*): chief of the Hathobards, Ingeld's father.

GARMUND (*Garmund*): Offa's father.

GEATS (*Geatas, Geotena*): a people of southern Sweden, the Gøtar, conquered by the Swedish kingdom in about the sixth century A.D. Infinite ink has been spilled about the precise identification of this people, and their homeland; any and all Old English editions of *Beowulf* (or a fine compendium like R. W. Chambers' *Beowulf*) can lead the interested reader as far as—and probably further than—he cares to go.

GOTHS (*Gifðas*): I have here substituted the well-known Goths for their virtually unknown cousins, the *Gifðas*. The latter tribe emigrated from lands near the mouth of the Vistula (a river in Poland) about the third century A.D., settled near the lower Danube, and were wiped out as an independent political entity by the Lombards, toward the end of the sixth century A.D.

GRENDEL (*Grendel*): a man-eating monster who terrorizes the Danes until killed by Beowulf. Grendel lives, with his equally monstrous mother, at the bottom of a foul lake inhabited by assorted other monsters; he is descended from Cain (the progenitor of all evil spirits), though his precise genealogy is not given. The etymology of his name is conjectural: it is perhaps related to Old Norse *grindill*, "storm," and *grenja*, "to bellow," and to other words meaning "sand," "ground (bottom) of a body of water," and "grinder (destroyer)."

HALGA (*Halga*): a Danish prince, third son of Healfdane, younger brother of King Hrothgar, and father of Hrothulf. Halga predeceased King Hrothgar by some twenty years. The epithet "good" may have been given him for strictly metrical reasons; nothing in the poem explains it.

HAMA (*Hama*): a character in the cycle of stories about Ermric (and Theodoric, not mentioned in *Beowulf*). Precisely what role Hama is supposed to have played, in the poem's oblique reference to him, is not understood.

HARETH (*Hæreð*): Higd's father, apparently a prosperous man of standing.

HATHCYN (*Hæðcyn*): a king of the Geats, Hrethel's second son, who ascends the throne after he accidentally kills his older brother, Herbald, and their father has died of grief. Hathcyn is killed by Ongentho, king of the Swedes, in a war which then sees Ongentho killed by a second band of Geats, led by Higlac.

HATHLAF (*Heaþolaf*): a Wulfing warrior, slain by Edgetho; his death causes a feud which is settled, after

Glossary of Names

Edgetho has been exiled, by the intercession (and gold) of Hrothgar.

HATHOBARDS (*Heaðobeardan*): a seafaring German tribe, sometimes identified with the Lombards (who had not yet migrated down toward Italy), sometimes with the Erulians, but not definitely placed either historically or geographically. They may have lived, at least for a time, on the south Baltic coast.

HEALFDANE (*Healfdene*): a Danish king, Beo's son, and father of Hergar, Hrothgar, Halga, and Urs. Whether or not the name means Half-Dane is uncertain.

HEMMING (*Hemming*): a kinsman of Offa, though in what precise relationship is not known.

HENGEST (*Hengest*): a Danish warrior, Hnaf's chief lieutenant and, de facto, his successor.

HERBALD (*Herebeald*): a prince of the Geats, Hrethel's oldest son. He is killed, in a hunting accident, by his brother, Hathcyn, and his necessarily unavenged death causes his father to die of grief. The parallel with the Balder (Baldr) myth has often been noted.

HERDRED (*Heardred*): a king of the Geats, Higlac's son, killed by the powerful Swedish king, Onela.

HERGAR (*Heorogar*): a Danish king, oldest son of Healfdane, older brother and predecessor of Hrothgar, and father of Herward. His reign was apparently a brief one.

HERMOD (*Heremod*): an archetypal but partly historical Danish king, of great military prowess combined with the lowest possible character. Like Wayland, the famous smith, Hermod is mentioned frequently in the poetry of other Germanic languages.

HEROT (*Heorot*): the lofty battle hall built by King

Hrothgar, to celebrate his victories, house his growing band of followers, and perhaps to perpetuate his fame. As the poet hints, in lines 84–85, a coming war will result in the burning down of Herot.

HERWARD (*Heoroweard*): Hergar's son. He seems to have been bypassed, at his father's death (his uncle Hrothgar taking the throne), either because he was thought too young to rule or because he had been out of favor with his father. See lines 2160–2162, and see under Hrothulf, below.

HIGD (*Hygd*): Higlac's wife, Hareth's daughter. Her name means "thoughtful," or "prudent."

HIGLAC (*Hygelac, Higelac*): a king of the Geats, Hrethel's son, younger brother of Herbald and Hathcyn. Higlac is both Beowulf's feudal lord and his uncle.

HNAF (*Hnæf*): a Danish king, killed by Finn; his sister was Finn's wife.

HONDSHEW (*Hondscioh*): a Geat warrior, one of Beowulf's companions on the journey to King Hrothgar's court. Hondshew is the man killed and eaten by Grendel, on the evening when the Geats instead of the Danes lay sleeping in Herot, Hrothgar's hall—the evening when Beowulf, instead of becoming the monster's second victim, gave Grendel his mortal wound.

HRETHEL (*Hreðel*): a king of the Geats, Higlac's father, Beowulf's grandfather.

HRETHRIC (*Hreðric*): the older of Hrothgar's two young sons.

HROTHGAR (*Hroðgar*): a Danish king, second son of Healfdane, builder of Herot, and beneficiary of Beowulf's courage. One of the principal characters of the poem, he is depicted as near the end of his life, wise, brave, but troubled, remembering his glorious past, afflicted with first Grendel and then Grendel's monstrous mother, and worried about the fate of his sons, at his nephew Hrothulf's hands, after his imminent death. Hrothgar has befriended Beowulf's father, which more than satisfactorily accounts for the help Beowulf gives him.

HROTHMUND (*Hroðmund*): the younger of Hrothgar's two young sons.

HROTHULF (*Hroðulf*): Halga's son, Hrothgar's nephew. Although Welthow, Hrothgar's queen, invokes the spirit of goodwill prevailing at the Danish court, and predicts that Hrothulf will guard her two young sons, the Anglo-Saxon listener knew that Hrothulf was later to seize the throne, after Hrothgar's death, and also was to murder Hrethric, Hrothgar's legal heir. Hrothulf, the Anglo-Saxon listener knew further, was subsequently to be killed by Hergar's son, Herward—but none of this is stated in the poem.

HRUNTING (*Hrunting*): Unferth's ancient sword. Few things show more clearly the importance of weapons (and armor), in Anglo-Saxon culture, than their being assigned names—and, on occasion, other personalized characteristics.

INGELD (*Ingeld*): a prince of the Hathobards, Froda's son, married to Freaw, the Danish princess.

JUTES (*Eotan*): a Frisian people, or a people allied with (and possibly subordinate to?) the Frisians.

NAGLING (*Nægling*): the name of Beowulf's sword. See under Hrunting, above.

OFFA (*Offa*): a king of the Angles—those of them who did not migrate to Angle-land (England) but remained on the European continent. Offa is the husband and tamer of Thrith. Various historical and mythological narratives are fused in this briefly told tale. (See also the Old English poem "Widsith.")

ONELA (*Onela*): a Swedish king, younger son of Ongentho, and husband of the Danish king Healfdane's daughter. Onela seized the Swedish throne, after his older brother's death; his brother's sons fled to Herdred, king of the Geats. The Swedish king thereupon invaded Geatland, killed Herdred and the older of his two nephews (the legal heir to the Swedish throne), but then returned home and permitted Beowulf to rule Geatland. However, Beowulf soon supported an invasion of Sweden by the surviving nephew, and the latter took both Onela's life and his throne. The poet regards Onela as something of a model king.

ONGENTHO (*Ongenþeow*): a Swedish king, mighty in battle, and obviously respected by the poet. In the fighting which followed Hrethel's death, Ongentho first killed Hathcyn, the Geats' king, and was then himself killed by another group of Geats, led by Higlac. Ongentho is Onela's father.

RENNSBURG (*Hreosnabeorh*): the location of the battle between Swedes and Geats, in which first Hathcyn and then Ongentho are killed.

SHILD (*Scyld*): a Danish king, Beo's father, Healfdane's grandfather, and Hrothgar's great-grandfather. Shild is mythological; he has Scandinavian analogues, as Skjǫldr, and scholars have elaborated a variety of possible religious/agricultural meanings for his story.

SIEGMUND (*Sigemund*): son of Vels, father (and uncle) of Fitla. This is the *Nibelungenlied* (and Wagner's) Siegmund in one of his assorted other incarnations.

SWERTING (*Swerting*): Higlac's grandfather.

THRITH (*þryð, Modþryðo*): Offa's wife, and a type of haughty, violent young woman very like Katharina, in Shakespeare's *The Taming of the Shrew*. Like Katharina, Thrith is tamed and gentled by a husband stronger

Glossary of Names

even than she; unlike *The Taming of the Shr*... poem does not tell us precisely how the miracle... accomplished.

UNFERTH (*Unferð*): one of Hrothgar's courtiers, skillful with words, and also a man of considerable reputation as a warrior; his father is Ecglaf. Unferth's sword, lent to Beowulf for the fight with Grendel's mother, is called Hrunting.

VELS (*Wæls*): Siegmund's father. The familial name is, in this version of the story, derived from Vǫlsung, in the Norse saga.

WAYLAND (*Weland*): a smith celebrated in many surviving Germanic poems; to ascribe a sword or a mail shirt to his gifted hammer was to evoke an automatic association of wonderful workmanship and, in most cases, also of wonderful men and deeds. Wayland is mentioned at some length in "Deor," perhaps the oldest surviving Old English poem. (see Raffel, *Poems from the Old English* [1960], pp. 39–40.)

WELTHOW (*Wealhþeow*): Hrothgar's queen, and the mother of his young sons, Hrethric and Hrothmund. Most of her speeches are full of tragic implications, well-known to the Anglo-Saxon audience. See under Hrothulf, above.

WEXSTAN (*Wihstan, Weohstan*): Wiglaf's father, and more or less vaguely related to Beowulf. Wexstan killed the older of Onela's nephews, when that Swedish king invaded Geatland, but whether he was himself a Swede, or a Geat serving the Swedes, is not known. In any case, after the survivor of Onela's two nephews returned to Sweden, killed Onela, and became king, Wexstan could not (and did not) remain in Sweden.

WIGLAF (*Wiglaf*): a Geat warrior, more or less vaguely related to Beowulf, possibly having some Swedish blood; his father is Wexstan. Chosen to accompany Beowulf to the aged hero's fight with the dragon, Wiglaf is the only member of a presumably select band who goes to Beowulf's help. He seems to have become king, after Beowulf's death.

WULF (*Wulf*): a Geat warrior, Efor's brother.

WULFGAR (*Wulfgar*): Hrothgar's herald. The precise familial link which leads the poet to call him "a prince born to the Swedes" (*þæt wæs Wendla leod*) is missing.

WULFINGS (*Wylfingas*): a Germanic tribe, probably resident south of the Baltic Sea. Welthow, Hrothgar's queen, may have been a Wulfing.

YRS (*Yrse*): daughter of Healfdane. Her name is not actually given in the manuscript; despite the high degree of probability, editors have hesitated to fill the gap with anything more than [ ] and a footnote. A translator must either gamble or evade.

GENEALOGIES

THE GEATS

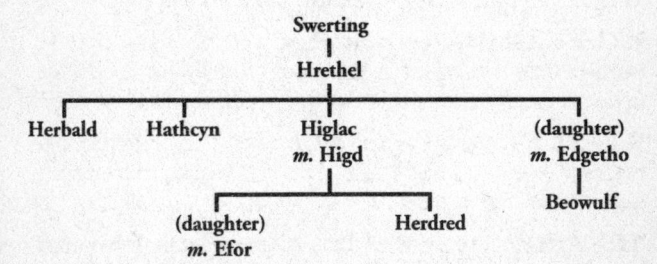

Swerting
Hrethel

- Herbald
- Hathcyn
- Higlac *m.* Higd
  - (daughter) *m.* Efor
  - Herdred
- (daughter) *m.* Edgetho
  - Beowulf

THE DANES

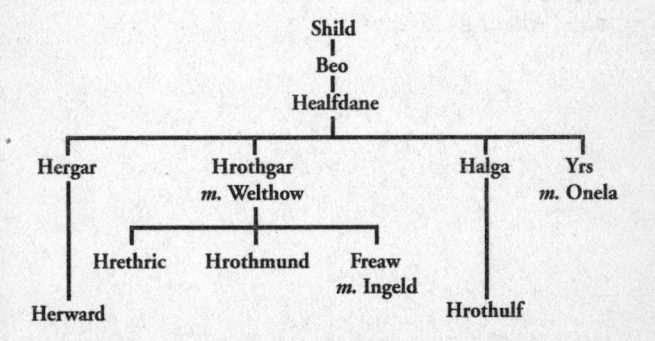

Shild
Beo
Healfdane

- Hergar
  - Herward
- Hrothgar *m.* Welthow
  - Hrethric
  - Hrothmund
  - Freaw *m.* Ingeld
- Halga
  - Hrothulf
- Yrs *m.* Onela

THE SWEDES

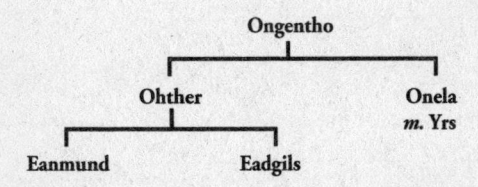

Ongentho

- Ohther
  - Eanmund
  - Eadgils
- Onela *m.* Yrs

Afterword

This translation of *Beowulf* first appeared in 1963. That year witnessed Martin Luther King's "I Have a Dream" speech in Washington, D.C., and President John F. Kennedy's assassination in Dallas, the beatitude of Thelonious Monk at the piano and a scalp-tingling Barbra Streisand singing "Bewitched, Bothered, and Bewildered." It saw the first miniskirt, the first five-digit ZIP code, and the first woman in space. The Beatles declared "I Want to Hold Your Hand," and Bob Dylan, with faked Woody Guthrie accents, "Don't Think Twice, It's All Right." Hollywood's creative energy peaked and in a few miraculous months produced *Tom Jones*, *Hud*, *From Russia with Love*, *The Birds*, *Cleopatra*, *The Leopard*, *Dr. Strangelove*, *It's a Mad, Mad, Mad, Mad World*, and *Charade*. In Vietnam, President Ngo Dinh Diem and his brother were killed in a military coup. The vivid rendering of *Beowulf* by Burton Raffel has held up well over the past half century or so—better, indeed, than many of its original readers.

Raffel's assertion in his Introduction that we were lucky to have *Beowulf*, that it was "great poetry" and not cruel and unusual punishment, was necessary in a world of youthful demographics and set examination texts. Kingsley Amis, preparing for his Oxford finals, had blasted *Beowulf* as an "anonymous, crass, purblind, infantile, featureless heap of gangrened elephant's sputum." And in *Annie Hall* (1977), Woody Allen was still advising a college-bound Diane Keaton: "Just don't take any course where they make you read *Beowulf*." How quickly things change. *Beowulf* is no longer on the endangered-species list. The poem has been breeding vigorously, spawning an exaltation of films, operas, puppet shows, animated cartoons, comic books, readings, staged musicals, and video and board games. Many of these remakes have a lot to answer for. In the most recent film version (2007), a gross, scaly, mucus-drooling, cadaverous Grendel roars and rips and pops people like pills. His mother, a slinky femme fatale with otherworldly curves (Angelina Jolie), rises naked from the mere, dripping liquid gold onto her stiletto heels, wooing Beowulf (a computer-enhanced Ray Winstone) with lines like: "I know that, underneath your glamour, you're as much a monster as my son, Grendel." The great Danes grunt, drink, belch, chant, and fight in the high hall, rugby boors whose private habits your high school teacher would not want you to think about.

Scholarly tradition wants us to speak well of the works we study. But an Afterword must not proclaim too loudly that the original Old English poem is far more powerful and moving than its modernizations, far more fun and accessible and meaningful (whether to get in touch with your inner hero or for improving your SAT scores). Such protestations might suggest that there is a point to the opposite argument: that the real *Beowulf* is tedious, elitist, and irrelevant to the world today. We do not want to hear too much about the evil lurking within our precincts, or about the art of losing without flinching.

Beowulf is a comparatively recent arrival in the hall of fame of English poetry. It was not until the end of the eighteenth century that scholars began to make sense of the charred and scorched manuscript and not until well into the nineteenth that *Beowulf* reached a wider audience. The poem was unknown to Chaucer,

Spenser, Shakespeare, Milton, Pope, Byron, and Keats. The prose synopsis offered in the 1 May 1858 issue of *Household Words*, edited by Charles Dickens, marks the poem's entry into public consciousness, in a world that did not mind as much as we do its "robust" attitudes to pastimes such as fighting, killing, and drinking. But *Beowulf* is a visitor from a distant land, a stranger whose words, idioms, grammar, gestures, and images we struggle to understand. Students of *Beowulf* have to accept a burden of ignorance about matters of authorship and chronology, composition, patronage, and transmission that would be intolerable to those who work in other periods of literary history. The poem gives few intelligible or adequate answers to ordinary literary questions about style, indebtedness, school, genre, performance, theme, or structure. And what we don't know hurts us. *Beowulf* is a text from the past in the past's own voice. It matters whether the poem, when new, was close to its oral roots, or whether it was a nostalgic reconstruction of a Northern heroic age. It matters whether *Beowulf* was a prop by which an aristocratic ideology established itself in a society not so different from that portrayed in the poem, or whether it was a late, culturally charged act of repetition, imaginatively reconciling its readers to new realities. It matters "whodunit" and when and how.

Scholars agree on a few chronological boundaries, forming a triptych: first, the time and place of the poem's action, the late fifth and sixth centuries in East Scandinavia, chiefly around the shores of the Kattegat (England is never mentioned, an awkward omission for the first native English "epic"); then the moment of composition, some time between the middle of the seventh century and the beginning of the eleventh, when an English poet, looking back, told of an age of Northern kings and retainers long gone; and, finally, the date of the sole surviving manuscript, into which two scribes, probably in the decade after 1000, copied the poem we call *Beowulf*. The breadth of the middle panel—a three-and-one-half-century window of opportunity—is both unattractive and worrisome, but then no other long Old English poem can be confidently situated before the tenth century.

As poetry, *Beowulf* holds our interest because it is extraordinary, a strange and enchanting offspring of the real and the dreamworld, of Clio and Morpheus. The unknown compiler of the extant manuscript apparently had an interest in monsters: uncanny creatures stalk singly or in packs through the works he anthologized. *The Wonders of the East*, which precedes *Beowulf* in the codex, illustrates thirty-two marvels. Here are dragons, one hundred fifty feet long and as thick as stone pillars; huge cannibals with long legs and feet; and thirteen-foot-tall marble-white women accessorized with boar tusks, camel hooves, and oxtails. Beowulf's own beloved lord and uncle, Hygelac king of the Geats, was so gigantic that he, too, appears in a catalogue of monstrosities: no horse was strong enough to carry him, and after his death at the mouth of the Rhine, his bones were preserved for travelers to gawk at. The historian Gregory of Tours (d. 594) notes a raid on Frankish territory by the same Hygelac and dates it around the year 520. For some reason the *Beowulf* poet alludes at least four times to this fatal expedition, as if it were an anchor or touchstone, a way of breaking into and entering the past.

Readers coming to *Beowulf* for the first time are faced with a barrage of unfamiliar personal names (mostly beginning with H) and bewildered by an absence of clear reference points. Carthage stirs certain associations, but not Heorot. Who in the world is Hama, and what does Ingeld have to do with anything? The names and deeds of Odysseus and Penelope, Agamemnon and Helen, Aeneas and Dido, ring bells: they and the Greek and Roman classics are part of our cultural heritage. But Hrothgar, Healfdane, Hergar,

Halga, Hrethel, Hrethric, Herdred, Heatholaf, Hrothmund, Hrothulf, Hemming, Herbeald, Herward, Hildeburh, Hareth, and Higlac are total strangers. The Northern legends featured in *Beowulf* and taken for granted as belonging to both the poet and his public vanished from English memory soon after the Norman Conquest. We need to learn these stories in order to follow the poet's channel surfing, when he suddenly switches from the main narrative to another story, and then another, before returning. In *Beowulf*, these "digressions" are used in an allusive, referential way. To the Anglo-Saxons, the pleasure of recognition, of sharing in an erudite game, seems to have been as important as to readers of Ovid and Milton. Scandinavian story was something you had to know, like chess, claret, or cricket, if you wanted to be thought cultured. Some twenty different legends are alluded to by the poet. Most of the stories related have to do with the fall of a leader, an underdog's defiant resistance, the automaticity of revenge (called by Auden the earth's only perpetual motion machine), and the sorrow of lonely queens. Beowulf's own memory reaches back two generations, tracing the complex origins of the feud between the Swedes and the Geats. He can also forecast the feuds of the next generation: on the basis of a piece of information picked up at the Danish court, he turns the Ingeld legend into a political prophecy, a sequence of events likely to occur in the near future. Sometimes myth is pressed into service as history: Beowulf's story of Hathcyn's accidental slaying of Herbald seems to echo a fratricide in the Norse pantheon, the god Hothr's unwitting killing of Baldr. When the poet mentions earlier heroes of legend like Scyld, Heremod, Finn, Offa, Sigemund, Ermanaric, and Hama, he does not make them contemporaneous with the sixth-century events described, but sets them in a distant mirror, conveying the illusion of a many-storied long ago. His reconstruction of a Northern heroic age presents such an internally consistent picture of Scandinavian society around AD 500 that his imitation of historical truth has been taken for the reality.

One historical context for *Beowulf* that has enriched our view of the poem in recent years is archaeology. The excavation of the richly furnished Sutton Hoo ship burial in 1939 provided sufficient treasure, arms and armor, drinking vessels, and exotic precious goods to show that the poet need not have been fantasizing about the wealth of the early North. The material culture of seventh-century Sussex came to look very like that depicted in the poem, give or take a garnet or two. (When you have *one* early epic and *one* lavish ship burial, the temptation to marry the two is strong.) Excavations in the 1950s of a seventh-century site at Yeavering in Northumbria revealed large timber halls very like Hrothgar's Herot. The trouble is that most of these items—from cremations and ship burials to helmets, swords, and wooden buildings—are not tied to any one time or place and can be found somewhere in the North during most of the first millennium AD. The historical Herot has often and plausibly been localized near the village of Lejre on the Danish island of Zealand. (Thietmar of Merseburg, writing in 1013–18, described Lejre as the former "capital of the kingdom.") Beginning in the late 1980s, and again in 2004–5, excavations at Lejre began to uncover the remains of a series of structures dating from the mid-sixth century to the late-tenth century, halls pretty much where and when legend said they should be, and far larger than anything so far excavated in England. It could have been in such a great central place, or so it is pleasant to speculate, that the Danish *scops* or "oral singers" depicted in *Beowulf* recited their legendary tales and songs of praise (88–98, 495–97, 853–97, 1063–1159). But just because fifth- or sixth-century Danes were imagined to behave this way does not mean that song in the high hall was how *Beowulf* itself was propagated.

Beowulf is a hero, demonstrating resolution and fortitude in the face of demonic and human enemies alike. His are the virtues of a warrior aristocracy, and he knows the lingo: "Each of us must experience the end of life in the world," he tells the Danes quaking in the hall; "let him who is permitted achieve fame before death. That is for a slain warrior the best there is." Beowulf's victories are praised by all onlookers, including the narrator: he was "the strongest of warriors," "the strongest in might on that day of this life." His loyalty, munificence, wisdom, and nobility are extolled; so, too, are the eloquent formal speeches in which he makes his qualities of mind and heart known. "He held to his high destiny," says Wiglaf of his slain leader, "of all men in the world he was the most glorious warrior." The last word in the poem is uttered by Beowulf's mourners, who commend their slain leader as "keenest to win glory."

If *Beowulf* is widely hailed today as the first great masterpiece of English poetry, it probably has less to do with its hero's might than its poet's melancholy. Few today automatically assume that fighting is glorious or even fun. The poem's heroic fellowship is precarious, a bright hall haunted by menace. Scenes of rejoicing are swiftly undercut by forecasts of disaster; alliterative pairings such as *æfter wiste . . . wop* "after the feast . . . weeping" and *gyrn æfter gomene* "sorrow after joy" are dark, mocking refrains. The sadness, the poignancy, the downbeat that we associate with *Beowulf* come from the epic poet's sense of duration, how time condemns itself and all human endeavor. Herot, like Troy, will be snuffed out by flames and only its memory will linger for a while.

One hallmark of a fine poetic translation is that it makes readers curious about the nature of the original. Unlike Raffel's vivid concreteness, Old English verse is composed in a highly patterned, formulaic style, studded with vagueness. But there are compensations: a single phrase, unremarkable, demanded by the meter, and exhausted by a chorus of previous poets, sometimes calls up a multitude of disparate and unexpected thoughts, the inferred unsaid, which in this poetry is often as important as the repeated just said. Longfellow was impressed by the lines in *Beowulf* in which a man mourns his son's death on the gallows (a melancholy scene if there ever was one). As the father looks upon his child's former dwelling, the sense of loss seems to be expressed on a more than individual scale. A word-for-word gloss follows this extract:

> Gesyhð sorhcearig on his suna bure,
> winsele westne, windge reste,
> reote berofene—ridend swefað,
> hæleð in hoðman; nis þær hearpan sweg,
> gomen in geardum, swylce ðær iu wæron.
> Gewiteð þonne on sealman, sorhleoð gæleð
> an æfter anum; þuhte him eall to rum,
> wongas ond wicstede.   (2455–62)

He looks, sorrow-mournful, upon his son's chamber, wine-hall deserted, windy rest, robbed of joy—riders sleep, men in grave; is not there harp's music, joy in dwelling, as once there had been. He goes then to couch, sorrow-song keens, lonely one for lone one; seemed to him all too spacious, fields and dwelling place.

The letters ð and þ represent the *th* sound in *that* and *thigh* respectively; æ represents the vowel sound in *cat*; all words except *gesyhð* and *gewiteð* are accented on the first syllable. Each verse consists of two half lines (normally with two stressed syllables each) linked by alliteration. The "little" words of Old English are still recognizable to speakers of modern English: pronouns such as "his," "him," and "all," adverbs such as "then," "too," and "there," prepositions such as "after," "on" and "in," and the conjunction "and." Other words in the passage above are related to modern English words: e.g., *bur* gave us "bower," *win-*, "wine," *sorh-*, "sorrow," *cearig*, "chary," *sunu*, "son," *hearpe*, "harp," *gomen*, "game," *geard*, "yard," *windig*, "windy," *rum*, "room," *rest*, "rest," *-stede*, "stead"; the verbal forms *is*, *wæron*, and *þuhte* correspond to "is," "were," and "thought" (as in "methought"). Still other words, especially those in the poetic register (e.g., *hæleð*, *wong*, *sele*) have disappeared from the language. Old English verse does without the articles "the" and "a," as I have in my literal gloss.

But even with the verse stripped of rhythm and sound and inflections, the words muted and tired, the passage is still recognizably poetry, touching the deep wellsprings of grief and loneliness, the temporality and finitude of an indifferent world. The father's (and poet's) eye moves from the corpse, the lifeless "bone house" riding on the gallows, to a windswept hall, its horsemen vanished—an emptied world and the awful spaciousness of things. The meaning of some words is uncertain (e.g., *hoðman*, *sealman*, *reote*); the compression of *an æfter anum*, untranslatable: "the one for the other" but also "the lonely one for the only one" (or vice versa); and the punctuation, modern and interpretive.

The poet's vagueness disturbs us. A recent translation turns "windy rest" (= resting place, repose, bed) into "the draughty fireplace where the wind is chattering," a concrete, homey image that appeals to current taste. But the Anglo-Saxon poet's nonvisual and reticent "windy rest" allowed his audience to recall other windy places: not only the "windswept walls" that form part of the "ruined hall" topos but also the grave on the hill, the wind-battered sea cliffs, the last defense of the land, and the "windy hall" in which Satan must endure eternity. The poet's sequence of images conveys with economy how, lacking one person, the man bereft lacks the whole world. But why these unidentified "riders," why "harp music"? The answer is that they, like hawk and mead cup, are poetic shorthand, calling up a whole complex of ideas associated with the transience of earthly joy. Two hundred lines earlier, the *Beowulf* poet described another empty hall in terms of absence: "There is no delight of the harp, joy of the mirth-wood, no good hawk flies through the hall, nor does the swift horse pound the courtyard." The speaker of the poem known as *The Wanderer* contemplates a ruined "wine hall," buffeted by winds, and says: "Where has the horse gone? Where has the man gone? ... Where are hall joys?" The fact that any piece of Old English verse is likely to resemble others means that the individual poem could hold its punches, letting its resonant formulas make the connections. "Riders" and "wind," "wine" and "harp" are loaded words, bearing traditional baggage that a poet had only to unpack, not invent.

So don't read *Beowulf*. Do something else, anything: paint your toenails, go to the mall, check the weather report, text message, contemplate a mole; at the mention of the heroic, shudder; return some DVDs, watch CNN news. And then, when the whole world seems as gray and flavorless as a latte left out in the rain, pick up your *Beowulf*, and yield yourself to its lonely fenland demons, drunken thanes in army blankets, and golden pagan hero.

—Roberta Frank

The Great Epic Poems

THE ILIAD
translated by W.H.D. Rouse
This very readable prose translation tells the tale of Achilles, Hector, Agamemnon, Paris, Helen, and all of Troy besieged by the mighty Greeks. It is a tale of glory and honor, of pride and pettiness, of friendship and sacrifice, of anger and revenge. In short, it is the quintessential western tale of men at war.

THE ODYSSEY
translated by W.H.D. Rouse
Kept away from his home and family for 20 years by war and malevolent gods, Odysseus returns to find his house in disarray. This is the story of his adventurous travels and his battle to reclaim what is rightfully his.

THE CANTERBURY TALES: A Selection
Geoffrey Chaucer
This unique edition maintains much of the middle English text, while at the same time incorporating normalized contemporary spellings to produce a text that is both easy to read and faithful to the sound and sense of Chaucer's original. This volume contains all of the most famous tales, from the mirthful to the bawdy to the profoundly moral, reflecting not only the manners and mores of medieval England, but indeed the full comic and tragic dimensions of life.

Available wherever books are sold or at
signetclassics.com

SIGNET CLASSICS

CLASSIC TALES OF
MEDIEVAL CHIVALRY

SIR GAWAIN AND THE GREEN KNIGHT
translated by Burton Raffel
A rich, poetic translation in verse of one of the great Arthurian texts from the Middle Ages. This is the tale of Gawain, Knight of the Round Table, and his strange and marvelous adventure at the court of the mysterious and magical Green Knight.

IDYLLS OF THE KING & Selected Poems
Alfred Lord Tennyson
Tennyson's dramatic retelling of the Legend of Arthur and his knights in poetic form. Both delightful and dramatic, this is Tennyson's masterpiece.

LE MORTE D'ARTHUR
Sir Thomas Malory
Sir Thomas Malory gathered together a number of disparate tales of Arthur and his Round Table and made them into one long work which is an exciting and entertaining tale. First printed in 1485, it has become the basis for most of the Arthurian narratives written since.

Available wherever books are sold or at
signetclassics.com

S400